BOLD PRIVATEERS

TERROR, PLUNDER AND PROFIT ON CANADA'S ATLANTIC COAST

ROGER MARSTERS

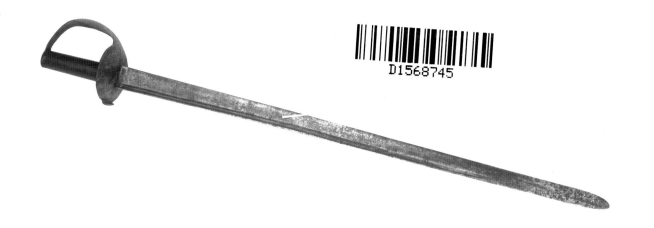

D1568745

FORMAC PUBLISHING COMPANY LIMITED

HALIFAX

Formac Publishing Company Limited acknowledges the support of the Cultural Affairs Section, Nova Scotia Department of Tourism and Culture. We acknowledge the financial support of the Government of Canada through the Book Publishing Industry Development Program (BPIDP) for our publishing activities.

We acknowledge the support of the Canadian Council for the Arts for our publishing program.

Library and Archives Canada Cataloguing in Publication

Marsters, Roger, 1966-
        Bold privateers : terror, plunder and profit on Canada's Atlantic coast / by Roger Marsters.

Includes bibliographical references and index.
ISBN 0-88780-644-9

        1. Privateering—History. I. Title.

KZ6573.M365 2004   910.4'5   C2004-905452-X

Formac Publishing Company Limited
5502 Atlantic Street
Halifax, Nova Scotia B3H 1G4
www.formac.ca

First published in the US in 2005:
Casemate
2114 Darby Road, 2nd Floor
Havertown, PA 19083

Printed and bound in Canada

CONTENTS

INTRODUCTION. 5

NEW FRANCE'S CHAMPION. 13

A CORSAIR ON THE BORDER. 25

BARON OF THE WILDERNESS. 37

THE ANCIENT WARRIOR. 45

A PRIVATEER'S MISFORTUNE. 53

A PRIVATEER IN THE NAVY. 63

SEA RANGER. 75

NOVA SCOTIA BESIEGED. 85

NOVA SCOTIANS ON THE SPANISH MAIN. 97

NEW ENGLAND'S SCOURGE. 105

NOVA SCOTIA'S MAN O' WAR. 117

BIBLIOGRAPHY. 126

INDEX. 127

Illustration Credits and Sources

Library and Archives Canada:
C-001020, Henri Beau (artist), 13L; C-001020, Henri Beau (artist), 14L; C-026026, Alfred Sandham (artist), 14R; C-000182, Henri Beau (artist), 16L; C-006007, 18R; C-6031, P. L. Morin, 18L; C-001916, Peter Rindisbacher (artist), 19; C-003686, 20R; C14045, 21L; C-012005, 22; C-030873, R. G. A. Levinge (artist), 30L; C-26026, 31R; C-21112, Jacques Grasset St.-Sauver (artist), 34; C-014861/C-014863, 36R; C-001321, Elbridge Knightley (artist), 37; C-023095, 38R; C-002525, James Meres (artist), 42 B; C-002706, John Hamilton (artist), 45; NMC 22499 (2 Sect), Etienne Verrier (artist), 50; C-006217, Mary E. Bonham (artist), 58R; NMC 14661, 58B; C-013314, Thomas Davies (artist), 60T; C-112058, Joshua Reynolds (artist), 61R; C-000577, Thomas Davies (artist), 62; C-041665, William Wynne Ryland (artist), 63T; C-000101, W. Ridgway (artist), 67T; C-001090, *From river mouth to Jemseg*, 68; C-000125, C.W. Jefferys (artist), 69; NMC 1829 (H12) NMC 816, John Rocque (artist), 72; C-000357, Richard Short (artist), 73 B; C-146039, Francis Swaine (artist), 73T; C-003916, Joseph Highmore (artist), 74T; C-002502, 74B; C-001226, 76L; C-142217, C-069902, 78R; Thomas Beach (artist), 79L; C-024549, Alfred Sandham (artist), 81R; C-073709, C.W. Jefferys (artist), 81L; C-003490, W.F. Mitchell (artist), 85; C-000277, Charles Randle (artist), 89T; C-013788, Alexander Cavalie Mercer (artist), 89B; C-002551, James S. Meres (artist), 96; C-111499 (cf. NSM), 101; NMC 1861 (H2), Thomas Jefferys (artist), 109R; C-100382, Charles Turner (artist), 117; C-007470, John T. Lee (artist), 118; C-041824, J. C. Schetky (artist), 119L; C-149998, 124.

Library of Congress:
LC-USZ62-54812, 17R; LC-USZ62-105732, Charles Delort, 66R; LC-USZ62-105952, Peter Canot, 83 B; cf. Dal, Leg. Library; LC-USZ62-126940, 56; LC-USZ62-19203, 91 R; LC-USZ62-31048, 103; LC-USZ62-38578, 47T; fr. *Gentleman's Magazine*, 1755; LC-USZ62-45303, 91L; LC-USZC2-1366, T/K, 88R; LC-USZC2-1855, Richard Paton, 93; LC-USZC4-4597, 28L; LC-USZCN4-29, 35; USZ62-96233, 39T; USZC4-737, T/K, 88L.

Nova Scotia Archives and Records Management:
Thomas Child (artist), 28R; 58L; 76R; Morse Print #45, 94L; Lunenburg, 94R; Artifacts Collection #52.20, 95B.

Réunion des Musées National/Art Resource New York:
ART147047, Louvre, Paris, 54T; ART151252, 23; ART156998, Chateau des Versailles, 32; ART184611, Louvre, Paris, 27; ART184618, Chateau des Versailles, 48; ART184622, Musée du Quai Branly, Paris, 46R; ART184626, Bibliothèque Nationale de l'Opera, 84; ART184847, Musée de la Marine, Paris, 44; Art184940, Musée de la Marine, Paris, 26.

Other Sources:
Art Gallery of Nova Scotia, 82R, 90, 98, 110, 120, 123.
Bowater Mersey, Liverpool, NS, *Rover* 99, *Liverpool Packet*, 107.
Centre de conservation du Québec, 42T.
Alaric and Gretchen Faulkner, *The French at Pentagoet 1635-1674* Augusta, Me. and Saint John, NB, 1987, (p. 123), 38L.

Andre Vachon, (p. 252) *Dreams of Empire: Canada Before 1700*, Ottawa, (1982), 15L, 15R.
Andre Vachon, (p.126) *Taking Root: Canada from 1700 to 1760*, Ottawa, (1985), 24, 29.
National Maritime Museum, Greenwich, *Launch of The Cambridge*, (artist) John Cleveley the Elder (1752), 63.
B. W. Bathe et al. *The Great Age of Sail*, Edita Lausanne, 1967, 33L, 100.
Chapin, Howard Millar, *Rhode Island Privateers in King George's War 1739-1748*, 55, 60B.
Dalhousie University Archive, William Inglis Coll., 1979-147.64, Lieut. H. Pooley, 95T
Gervis Frere-Cook, *Decorative Arts of the Mariner*, London (1966), 52.
Emmanuel Le Roy Ladurie. *L'ancien Régime*. Paris, (1991), 25, 41, 46L, 51.
Claude Farrere. *Histoire de la Marine Francaise*. Paris, (1934), 47B.
J. S. Virtue & Co. Ltd., Rathbone, Lieut. Chas. Rathbone, p.28, *Her Majesty's Navy including its deeds and battles*. London, 47L.
Howard Chapin, *Privateering in King George's War 1739-1748*, Providence, 1928, 64, 65B, 67B.
Richard Hough, (p.157) *Fighting Ships* (Putnam, 1967), 54B, 77.
Paul Lacroix, *XVIIme Siècle: Institutions, Usages et Costumes*. Paris, (1880), 13R, 17L, 30 R, 31B, 43.
Maritime Museum of the Atlantic, 112L.
S.E. Morison, *Maritime History of Massachusetts*, 108R.
National Gallery of Canada: 6268, Thomas Davies (artist), 71; 6270, Thomas Davies (artist), 83T; 6271, Thomas Davies (artist), 61R; Andre Vachon, (p.76) *Taking Root: Canada from 1700 to 1760*. Ottawa: 1985.
Nova Scotia Historical Society Collections, v.16 (1912), 105.
Nova Scotia Museum, 121; J. E. Woolford (c 1818), 122.
Parks/ Claude Joseph Vernet (10a209), 59.
Privateer Days Commission, 113, 115.
Jean-Pierre Proulx, *The Military History of Placentia: A Study of the French Fortifications*. Ottawa, (1979), 36L.
Queens County Museum, Liverpool, NS, 87, 109, 114, 115.
Reproductions by Loyalist Arms, 87, 109, 115.
Royal Ontario Museum, 958.14.4, 66L.
C. H. J. Snider, *Under the Red Jack*, 112R, 87T.
Oliver Warner, *Great Sea Battles*, Spring Books, (1973), 57, 92L, 92R.
Photography:
Yves Bellemare, 42T.
Gary Castle, 70, 112L, 121.
Friends of Colonial Pemaquid, Maine, 20L, 21R, 33R.
Roger Marsters, 40, 53, 80, 106 R, 106L, 108L, 39 B, 79R, 82L.
Scott Munn, 87B, 99, 107, 111, 114, 116, 109L; 119R.
Norman Munroe, 49 TL, 49 BR, 49TR.

INTRODUCTION

In the early summer of 1756 the schooner *Musketo* sailed southward from her homeport of Halifax, Nova Scotia, armed to make war on her enemies and profits for her owners. In May, Britain had declared war on France, formally opening a conflict that had smouldered in North America for at least a year. The formal declaration of the Seven Years' War freed colonial governors to issue licenses permitting private ships-of-war — privateers — to prey on the commerce of the enemy. Like a dog let off its leash, *Musketo* set a course for the West Indies — the richest hunting grounds in the hemisphere — where prizes deeply laden with sugar, rum,

View of York Fort.

coffee, tobacco, indigo, gold and silver crowded the balmy seas.

In the Caribbean *Musketo* wasted little time making prizes, soon overtaking a big round-bottomed merchantman and halting her with a few well-placed warning shots. The ship, it turned out, was the *Patience* out of Amsterdam, carrying a rich, mixed cargo from the island of St. Eustatia. She was not French at all, but Dutch. *Musketo*'s officers were disappointed, but undaunted. If *Patience*'s cargo were proved French property, she was as fair a prize as though she flew the French flag itself. The privateersmen set out to show that it was so.

Boarding the Dutch ship, *Musketo*'s officers lined up members of the crew one by one and clamped thumbscrews on their hands and on other sensitive parts of their bodies. A fiddler from the Nova Scotian ship played a jaunty tune, while his compatriots danced a groaning seaman across *Patience*'s deck, hoping to learn where the ship's papers and valuables were hidden. The privateersmen took money and belongings from the merchant sailors before assuming control of *Patience* and sailing her to Halifax, where the ship would, hopefully, be condemned and sold for their profit.

Back in their homeport, however, things did not proceed so merrily for *Musketo*'s men. When their case came before the town's Court of Vice Admiralty, a small portion of the *Patience*'s cargo of coffee and sugar was indeed judged to be French property. It was condemned and sold for the sum of £195. The ship itself, however, along with the bulk of its cargo, was found to be the property of Dutch citizens and was released. Worse, *Musketo*'s Captain, Matthew Pennell, and her second lieutenant, John Crowley, were convicted of torturing members of *Patience*'s crew. They were sentenced to make reparations to each and to pay the cost of the court case. In the end, *Musketo*'s Caribbean adventure proved anything but profitable.

The atrocious behaviour of *Musketo*'s crew is an apt illustration of the popular view of privateering as "legalized piracy." But its aftermath in Halifax's Court of Vice Admiralty paints a rather different picture: one of privateering as a state-sponsored, closely regulated and surprisingly even-handed form of private warfare. Indeed, throughout the long wars of the eighteenth century privateering was a legally prescribed way for European nations to increase their military strength in an economical fashion, at the same time offering their merchants opportunities for profits to replace those lost to wartime interruptions in trade. It was, in the phrase of one Canadian expert, "the merchant's way of waging war."

The nature of the trade is perhaps most clearly illustrated by British colonial practice. In Nova Scotia, for example, individuals or groups wishing to undertake a privateering cruise were required to petition the colonial governor for permission. If granted, a commission — or Letter of Marque — was issued authorising the holders to sail against the shipping of enemy nations under conditions laid down in minute detail by the British Admiralty. They were then required to post a very substantial sum of money as a bond ensuring they would abide by the terms of their commission. If they breached these terms, the bond would be forfeit. Courts of Vice Admiralty in major colonial ports interpreted and enforced the terms and conditions of privateers' commissions, and judged the legitimacy of the prizes they captured and brought home. As the owners of *Musketo* learned to their cost, these judgements by no means automatically favoured the commissioned privateer.

This book tells the stories of some of these private men of war. It follows the careers of Acadian and Nova Scotian sailors commissioned to make war on their enemies during the long wars between France and England in the course of the eighteenth century — the great age of fighting sail. Their bold and disciplined conduct shows how very far the region's privateers were from being pirates, and how varied and important their responsibilities were to the fortunes of their respective nations. It shows that on the wild maritime frontier

Portrait of Joseph Barss, Jr., master of Liverpool Packet, *Nova Scotia's most famous and successful privateer.*

The harbour and port of St. Malo.

Jones and Bonhamme Richard *engaging the enemy.*

of New England and Nova Scotia, where the presence of regular naval forces was sporadic and limited, private warships and their masters sometimes assumed the tasks normally carried out by national navies, and did so remarkably well.

Accordingly, in addition to the commercial privateersmen like those of the ill-fated *Musketo*, this book considers the work of other seamen: members of colonial sea militias and *armateurs* (French privateers who secured the use of royal warships for expeditions planned and executed on their own account), for example — who likewise sailed with official commissions, but often with quite different intentions from their mercantile compatriots. The roles of privateers and of navies overlapped to a considerable degree.

Brig Rover, *a privateering vessel.*

The long history of commissioned seafaring in the region occupied by today's Atlantic Canada covers the full spectrum of marine warfare, from the most mercenary commercial enterprise to the most patriotic and disciplined public service. One of Acadia's most successful and renowned corsairs (the French term for privateers) was Pierre Morpain, who learned his trade sailing out of Saint-Domingue, the West Indian "République des Aventuriers," modern-day Dominican Republic. Here privateering, or "*la flibuste*" as it was called, was often distinctly "piratical," a "loose roving way of life" in the words of English buccaneer William Dampier.

Flibustiers were often little more than bands of armed gunmen, afloat in the simplest of vessels, attacking the most vulnerable of targets. Their characteristic action was the "descent," an attack on a vulnerable coastal community which was then ransomed back to its inhabitants under threat of destruction. Despite his past as a *flibustier*, Morpain proved a principled and disciplined fighter who struggled for decades to protect Acadia from New England attack, and who rose to

Naval combat off Cap Lizard in Cornwall, won by the French fleet commanded by Dugay-Trouin and the Chevalier de Forbin, against five English war vessels, On October 21, 1702.

Introduction

hold important positions in the administration of the great French colonial port of Louisbourg. At the same time, the West Indian tradition of the "descent" served him well in the endless frontier skirmishes with New England, where privateers were nearly as likely to meet the enemy on land as at sea.

A typical — and terrifying — tactic of West Indian privateers was the armed descent on unsuspecting coastal towns.

The careers of men like Pierre Le Moyne d'Iberville also demonstrate how disciplined and responsible private men of war could be, and how great the consequences of their actions for the course of the European powers' imperial ambitions in America. After serving his apprenticeship as a young Canadian officer in the French fur-trading *Compagnie du Nord*'s expeditions against the rival Hudson's Bay Company, d'Iberville learned to navigate the hazardous waters of the French Court at Versailles, gaining powerful allies who helped him to establish himself as an *armateur*.

D'Iberville's expeditions spanned the extent of France's American empire: in 1694 he conquered the rich fur-trading post of York Fort on Hudson Bay and in 1706 he captured the rich West Indian islands of Saint Christopher and Nevis, sending waves of fear through all the British colonies of America. D'Iberville's far-flung exploits as a soldier and corsair, taking him from the Canadian north to the Gulf of Mexico, won him lasting fame as the greatest fighter New France ever produced.

The sea militias of the British American colonies — provincial navies that carried out a broad range of duties in regions where the regular service seldom ventured in force or stayed for long — fall somewhere between *flibustiers* and *armateurs* in the spectrum of commissioned seafaring.

Maintained through colonial governors by the Board of Trade, rather than by the Admiralty, sea militias helped settle fledgling colonies, protect their growing trade and maintain their most distant outposts. The career of Sylvanus Cobb well illustrates the nature of their work: possessing an encyclopaedic knowledge of the Nova Scotian coast, he spent years supporting the colony's young out-settlements and supplying military posts at Annapolis, Windsor and Cumberland. He sailed the Bay of Fundy tirelessly, intercepting smuggled stores bound for French forces and hunting enemy provocateurs. Grave tasks were entrusted to these irregular navies, as his roles in the attack of Fort Beauséjour and the expulsion of the Acadians show. Such acts lead some to contend that the sea militias were the colonies' single greatest contribution to the success of British arms in America during the eighteenth century.

The various shadings of the privateering spectrum were not entirely separate, one from another. Colonial militias sometimes worked closely — though usually unofficially — with ships of the Royal Navy. And while Royal Navy officers may have resented privateers as unwelcome competition for prize money (on which remuneration in the regular service, as among private men of war, largely depended), they nevertheless made eager use of the shipping intelligence privateers were required to give them.

11

At times personnel moved from one form of marine service to another. Captain John Rous began his career in New England privateers, preying on Spanish shipping during the 1739 War of Jenkin's Ear before commanding a vessel of the Massachusetts' provincial marine at the 1745 siege of Louisbourg. There, his conduct so impressed Commodore Sir Peter Warren that he was granted a commission in the Royal Navy, playing a vital role in Nova Scotia's defence before distinguishing himself in naval operations during the siege of Quebec in 1759. Rous's brilliant career was exceptional, but not unique.

The stories of Morpain, d'Iberville, Cobb, Rous and their contemporaries give glimpses into the variety of ways that private men of war operated in the region during the eighteenth century. But this book also shows what it was like to suffer at the hands of privateers in this period. From constant imperial skirmishing on the Acadia-New England frontier in the years straddling the turn of the century to American privateering attacks on the Nova Scotian coast during the War of 1812, the region suffered privateers' attacks as frequently as it perpetrated them. This was perhaps most evident during the American Revolutionary War, when a range of attackers — from the famous naval hero John Paul Jones to the paltriest bandits in open boats — attacked the "fourteenth colony," preying on its shipping and sacking its towns, from Lunenburg to Annapolis Royal.

The growth of Nova Scotia's most famous privateering port was spurred by the persistence and intensity of these attacks. Repeatedly pillaged during the war, Liverpool outfitted its first privateers during the American Revolution. Not until the decades straddling the turn of the nineteenth century, however, did the town launch its most famous ships, commanded by its most famous men. In the wars with Revolutionary and Napoleonic France and the War of 1812 ships with names such as *Rover*, *Liverpool Packet* and *Sir John Sherbrooke* — commanded by men such as Alexander Godfrey, Joseph Freeman and Joseph Barss — won lasting fame on the New England coast and in the distant Caribbean. Their stories have been retold many times, reflecting glory on the port they sailed from.

The later chapters of this book retell the saga of Liverpool privateering, a most remarkable period in Atlantic Canadian history. But it puts those stories into the wider context of private naval warfare practiced in the region over the course of the eighteenth century. My hope is that, viewed alongside the remarkable exploits of the Acadian corsairs, Canadian *armateurs*, colonial sea militias and Royal Navy officers, the extent of their achievements will be seen as the last example of a centuries-long tradition of public service — and private gain — enacted in the harsh seas of Canada's east coast.

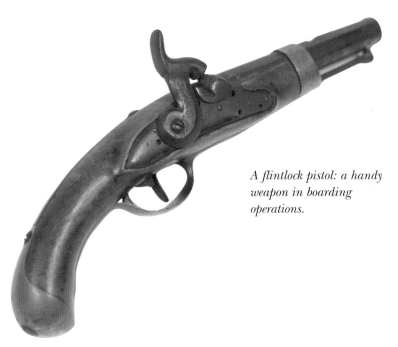

A flintlock pistol: a handy weapon in boarding operations.

Chapter One

NEW FRANCE'S CHAMPION

On an icy spring morning in early April 1686, 35 heavy, deeply laden bark canoes drove against the raging spring flood of the Ottawa River, voyaging west from the town of Montreal towards distant Lake Temiscaming and the unexplored lands beyond. In each boat three tough *voyageurs* — fighters and traders hardened to the rigours of wilderness travel — struggled to gain way against the current. At times they could neither paddle nor portage and were forced to drag their canoes through the icy water, neck-deep in places. Chilled, exhausted and constantly hungry from meagre rations, the men were mere weeks into a journey they knew would last

Left: Canadien fighter wearing snowshoes, or raquettes.
Right: The late seventeenth-century saw enormous growth of European merchant marines—and of navies to protect them.

months: an audacious overland military expedition from New France's heartland on the St. Lawrence River to distant James Bay, in the Canadian north. Outfitted by the French fur-trading *Compagnie du Nord*, their target was the commercial

Canadien fighters excelled at guerrilla fighting and ambush, often making long overland journeys to attack unsuspecting targets.

empire of England's Hudson's Bay Company, and control of the furs of 1.5 million square miles of northern America.

Among the expedition's officers were three Montreal brothers: Jacques Le Moyne de Sainte-Hélène, Paul Le Moyne de Maricourt, and Pierre Le Moyne d'Iberville. As the weeks passed, d'Iberville distinguished himself, showing great strength and courage. Swept away in a swollen river he almost drowned but soon recovered and resumed his arduous travels, undaunted. When hunger, fear and exhaustion drove the men ever closer to open mutiny, d'Iberville worked tirelessly to keep them moving and to keep them focused on the rich prizes at the river's end.

Pierre Le Moyne, Sieur d'Iberville: New France's boldest and most successful soldier.

When those prizes finally came in sight, d'Iberville didn't hesitate to take them.

In late June the force arrived at the Hudson's Bay Company post of Moose Fort on James Bay and attacked it, taking advantage of the complete surprise afforded by its overland journey. Entering the gate before the English defenders could close it, d'Iberville gained the interior of the fort. The English managed to close the gate behind him, cutting him off from his compatriots outside the palisade. Alone, surrounded by the enemy, he fought two-handed with sword and pistol, stabbing and slashing at his attackers. When the French finally reopened the gate they found d'Iberville

still holding his ground. Rushing to his aid, they overwhelmed the Hudson's Bay men and took the fort.

The taking of Moose Fort was one of a string of brilliant victories the *Compagnie du Nord*'s 1686 expedition for the commercial interests of France. The James Bay posts of Charles Fort and Albany Fort were captured too and more than 50,000 prime furs were plundered from the three posts. In the harbour off Charles Fort, d'Iberville showed a precocious talent for naval combat, leading boarding parties that took the English ship *Craven* by stealth, and taking captive John Bridgar, Company governor of the James Bay posts. It was an auspicious beginning to the military career of a man who soon proved to be New France's greatest soldier and corsair — a private naval man of war.

Pierre Le Moyne d'Iberville lived his life on the North American borderlands of France and England's commercial and imperial rivalry. He was born in Montreal in 1661, when the town was still a frontier post guarded from English and Iroquois attack by the Moulin du Côteau, a combined

Above: Fort Nelson was the linchpin of English power in the Canadian north.
Right: An ex-voto painting of d'Iberville, dedicated to his patron, Saint Anne.

Above left: A fanciful image of the warlike Frontenac, architect of France's strategy in North America, being carried into battle.
Above right: Members of religious orders—such as this Sulpician priest—were prominent in New France society.

gristmill and blockhouse. He studied with Montreal's Sulpician priests, learning Latin, rhetoric and the rudiments of military discipline. At age 12 he received both his first communion in the Roman Catholic Church and his first taste of warfare, joining an expedition to the western interior of the continent under New France's warlike governor Louis Buade de Frontenac. For the next 20 years d'Iberville's brilliant career as a soldier and *corsair* projected French imperial power to the remotest regions of America: from Montreal to the continental interior, from Newfoundland to

Havana and from Acadia to Hudson Bay.

In 1686 France and England skirmished repeatedly in Canada's James Bay, at a time when the two nations were formally at peace and when Catholic sovereigns — James II and Louis XIV — sat on the thrones of both countries. The skirmishes were entirely commercial in nature, the warlike overflow of competition between rival national fur-trading interests, the Hudson's Bay Company and the *Compagnie du Nord*. For the fighters who trekked to the distant Canadian north, the attacks were likewise a commercial proposition —

Louis XIV, the Sun King, whose hunger for glory set Europe and America aflame.

they fought chiefly for gain, rather than glory. In 1688, however, King James was deposed in favour of the arch-Protestant William of Orange in England's "Glorious Revolution." The nature of the struggle changed utterly, in Europe and America alike. Long-term commercial rivalries between colonial powers became increasingly intertwined with something approaching the status of a holy war.

The contest between France and England could not be confined to the furthest outposts of colonial empire indefinitely. It soon struck the borders of New France itself. Before dawn on August 5, 1689, 1500 Iroquois fighters, armed and encouraged by their English allies in New York, advanced northward through driving sleet to the settlement of Lachine, a few miles west of Montreal. Surrounding the village, they attacked mercilessly, burning houses, killing men, women and children. In all, nearly 100 people were killed or captured. For days afterward the Iroquois fighters ranged the countryside. Montreal was terrorized, and New France called for sharp, immediate action against the English colonies and their allies.

New France's governor, Frontenac, was keen to strike back at the heart of English power in America. He proposed an attack overland from Montreal to Manhattan, to divide the English from their Iroquois allies and isolate New England's northern frontier for eventual conquest. This plan was soon

William of Orange, the arch-protestant King of England.

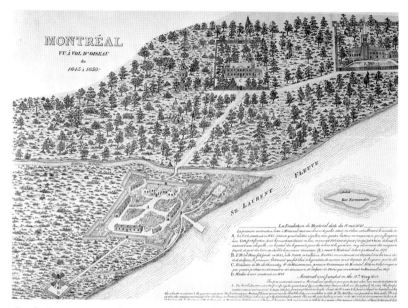

In the late seventeenth century Montreal was still a vulnerable frontier village, subject to repeated attack.

Nicolas d'Ailleboust de Manthet. D'Iberville was second in command. Setting out on snowshoes in bitter February cold, the heavily laden men lugged their gear — musket, hatchet, knife, bullet pouch and tobacco pouch, pack and blanket — through heavy snows across the frozen St. Lawrence and up the Richelieu River to Lake Champlain. After two weeks trudging through deep freeze and thaw, heavy snow and numbing slush, they arrived at Corlaer (modern-day Schenectady) the northernmost outpost of colonial New York.

As the war party approached on the night of February 18 the people of Corlaer slept soundly, lulled into security by the remoteness of their town and the lateness of the season. The palisade gates were left wide open, the ramparts unwatched. D'Iberville and his comrades entered the town undetected, surrounded the houses and attacked without warning, shooting, hacking and burning the townspeople in their beds

replaced by a simpler, more terrible one: the French and their native allies would stage unrelenting, merciless raids against the frontier settlements of northern New York and New England. What was sown at Lachine was reaped many times over at Salmon Falls, New Hampshire, Falmouth, Maine, and a dozen other isolated border villages. These obscure raids proved the opening gambits in a vast, bloody game — the winner-take-all battle of France and England for mastery of North America — that finally ended with the fall of Quebec some seventy years later.

D'Iberville returned from James Bay in early 1690, just in time to join Frontenac's raids against settlements in northern New York. The attacking force comprised 210 fighters — 114 Canadians and 96 natives — under the joint command of d'Iberville's brother Jacques Le Moyne de Saint-Hélène and

D'Iberville's bloody attack on Corlaer (Schenectady), N.Y., opened Frontenac's offensive against the English American colonies.

York Fort, like all posts on James and Hudson Bay, was best protected by its isolation. This was not a sufficient defense against bold and determined attackers such as d'Iberville.

as they awoke with terror. For two hours the assault continued in a chaos of blood, smoke and fire. The town was torched and 60 of the inhabitants were slaughtered outright. Another 25 were taken captive and taken on a forced march back to Montreal. The horrors of Lachine had been horribly avenged.

In July d'Iberville left the brutality of border warfare and returned to the sea. He had previously overwintered in James Bay in 1686-1687, returning to Quebec and to the north the following autumn in command of *Soleil d'Afrique*, a royal warship loaned to the *Compagnie du Nord* by the French crown. For years after 1690 he campaigned alternately in Hudson

A boarding axe, artefact from Fort Pemaquid.

western shore of Newfoundland's Avalon Peninsula. Following the Maine coast northeastward with a fleet of three ships, he encountered a squadron of English warships off Mount Desert Island and a chase ensued in light winds across the mouth of the Bay of Fundy. Doubling back to the coast under cover of darkness, d'Iberville succeeding in shaking his pursuers. The following day his ships took and ransomed several prizes before continuing to Plaisance, arriving in the settlement's sheltered anchorage on September 17.

Years of brutal border attacks made it increasingly clear

Bay and along the Acadia-New England coast, crossing and recrossing the Atlantic with instructions from the French court at Versailles. In 1691 his forces were too weak to take the Hudson's Bay Company's post at York Fort. In 1692 and again in 1693 he arrived too late in the season to campaign. In 1694 d'Iberville himself funded an expedition to the north, vowing a portion of the expected plunder for charitable works carried out in the name of his patron, Saint Anne. This year he at last laid siege to the rich prize of York Fort and though well provisioned and armed for a fight, the post promptly surrendered. The jubilant attackers renamed the post Fort Bourbon, overwintering there before returning to France with a rich cargo of captured furs.

D'Iberville's triumph was tempered by French losses in James Bay, and reversed when the English recaptured York Fort in 1696. But the *corsair* countered with a quick victory on the coast of Maine, providing naval support for the assault on the coastal strongpoint of Pemaquid. New England's northern frontier was now even more vulnerable to the French.

In early September 1696 d'Iberville ordered Pemaquid's stone fort reduced to rubble, then shaped a course for Plaisance, the French fishing and privateering base on the

The fisheries of Newfoundland and adjacent fishing banks—illustrated here—were one of the richest prizes in the European contest for North American mastery.

D'Iberville's martial career took him to the farthest reaches of France's American empire: from Hudson Bay to Newfoundland, Avadia to the Gulf of Mexico.

that there was only room for one European empire in North America. D'Iberville's Newfoundland campaign, the harshest and most thorough of his career, emphasized the point. The Grand Banks fishery — like the fur trade of the interior — was extremely lucrative, so it was a prime target in the struggle for American mastery. At this time the French Newfoundland fleet included some 400 ships and 18,000 men, serviced by a single Newfoundland base at Plaisance, with a resident

population of about 200. The huge English fishery, by contrast, was supported by at least three dozen shore settlements scattered along the eastern and northern coasts of the Avalon Peninsula, home to perhaps 2000 men, women and children. To disrupt the English fishery, these settlements had to be destroyed.

The campaign against the English in Newfoundland took the familiar form of a joint land-sea attack with d'Iberville leading the ground forces — 125 Canadian fighters and their First Nations allies. Plaisance's governor, Jacques-François de Mombeton de Brouillan, commanded the seaward force of 100 French fighters. Following his experiences at James Bay and Corlaer, d'Iberville approached his targets from the barren, uncharted interior of the Avalon, departing Plaisance on November 1. He rendezvoused with de Brouillan's force near the outpost of Ferryland nine days later and systematically sacked the settlements of Renews, Bay Bulls and Petty Harbour before proceeding to St. John's. By the end of the month the French were in sight of the capital, advancing blindly through a snowstorm with their plunder on their backs.

Cannon balls, artefacts from Fort Pemaquid.

Survivors of d'Iberville's crew struggle to get ashore after Pelican *grounds at York Fort.*

annihilation, St. John's surrendered and was put to the torch.

The expedition's swift and relentless advance continued. Leaving St. John's on January 17, 1697, the French took Harbour Grace, with 100 prisoners; they burned Brigus, leaving the population homeless in midwinter; they sacked Sibley's Cove, Hants Harbour, New Perlican and Hearts Content; and they burned Carbonear and the settlements on Random Sound. In all 27 outports were destroyed, 200 English settlers killed, 700 prisoners seized, and fortunes in codfish and property plundered.

Leaving Newfoundland in the 50-gun French frigate *Pélican* in July 1697, d'Iberville joined the frigates *Profond* and *Palmier* to cruise against York Fort on the barren western shores of Hudson's Bay, with brilliant results. On September 4 *Pélican* anchored in the mouth of the Hayes River, downstream from the Hudson's Bay Company's post of York Fort. The ships of the Company's annual fleet — *Hampshire*, 56 guns, *Dering*, 36 guns and *Hudson's Bay*, 32 guns — arrived off the anchorage soon after, laden with stores for the garrison of Company employees guarding the year's produce, thousands of rich furs, warehoused just upriver. Boldly and

In 1696 the town of St. John's was loosely strung out along the shore of its deep, enclosed harbour, sheltering some 160 men and their families under the meagre protection of three crude, undermanned forts. When the French expedition arrived, townspeople sheltered in the forts and ships in harbour, hoping the Royal Navy would come to their rescue. It didn't come soon enough. The French brought forward artillery and prepared a bombardment. Threatened with against the odds, *Pélican* upped anchor and sailed out to meet them the next day.

Pierre Le Moyne d'Iberville et d'Ardillières, New France's boldest soldier and *corsair* was *Pélican*'s master. He knew the northern seas well from previous campaigns. York Fort was a crucial post, funnelling the furs of North America to the markets of Europe. D'Iberville had attacked it, and taken it, before. This time he commanded a fleet of three frigates; soon, however, *Pélican* had been separated from her sisters in heavy ice.

When d'Iberville sailed out to challenge the enemy on the fifth, his ship was dangerously undermanned and his crew was ravaged by scurvy. Six of his guns wouldn't fire. The Company's ships formed up in line of battle, closing with *Pélican*, the powerful *Hampshire* at their head. As the opposing forces

Louisiana was planted as an anchor for France's American possessions. La Salle's 1684 expedition paved the way for d'Iberville and his successors.

drew close the English ship sheared off to avoid being boarded. D'Iberville immediately loosed a broadside at the next ship in line, *Dering*, tearing up her sails and rigging. Next he raked *Hudson's Bay* as she coasted into range. *Hampshire* returned and opened fire, damaging *Pélican*'s rigging and punching holes in her hull below the waterline.

The battle raged for three hours. At one point, as *Pélican* closed with *Hampshire*, the opposing captains paused in the smoke and roar of battle to toast one another's courage. *Hampshire* then raked *Pélican* with grapeshot, eviscerating men caught on the frigate's open deck. *Pélican* was holed seven times, her rigging shambled, her crew decimated by the enemy's gunnery. As the English at last closed to board his stricken ship, d'Iberville loosed a point-blank broadside into *Hampshire's* hull, striking it below the waterline. The English ship rolled over and slid beneath the freezing waters of the bay. D'Iberville then turned his attention to *Hudson's Bay*. She immediately struck her colours. *Dering*, belying her name, abandoned the fight and escaped offshore.

Pélican won the battle, but her ordeal was far from over. The ship was a scene of horror, littered with cannon shot, jagged splinters and wrecked gear, loud with the moans and screams of seamen maimed in the fight. As night fell a gale blew up, coating the decks with ice and driving the ship ever closer to the low, rocky shore. The crew tried to work *Pélican* offshore in the face of the rising storm but the ship lost her rudder and was driven back helplessly against the gale and rising tide. Working desperately, they launched the ship's surviving boats and jury-rigged rafts from shattered timber, abandoning the doomed ship and forcing their way through the roaring, frigid surf. Eighteen men died between the stricken ship and shore. *Hudson's Bay* likewise broke up in the night and was cast up onshore.

Three days later *Pélican's* sisters *Profond* and *Palmier* anchored off Hayes River, finding d'Iberville and his surviving crew and a coast littered with debris from the battle. Their crews promptly landed siege guns and moved them within range of the post. Hudson's Bay Company posts relied on their extreme isolation in the far north of the continent for their defence. The forts themselves were not strong: often little more than palisaded warehouses staffed by aging clerks. So, when d'Iberville's men advanced to besiege York Fort they were no doubt concerned to find it armed with serious artillery: two mortars, thirty-four large cannon, seven small cannon and several swivel guns. Their concern was misplaced. The French opened their bombardment on September 12. On September 13 York Fort surrendered, its rattled garrison refusing outright to fight on. D'Iberville's

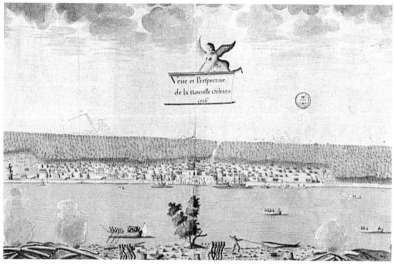

D'Iberville planted the seeds of the French presence on the Gulf of Mexico. Its richest fruit: New Orleans.

bold, desperate fight had, for the time being, won the fur trade of the vast interior of America for France.

In the years before his death in 1706 d'Iberville planted colonies at the mouth of the Mississippi and commanded expeditions sacking the rich West Indian islands of Saint Christopher and Nevis, terrorizing the English American colonies. None of his victories would endure, however, without France's determination to protect them. In the fall of 1697 the Treaty of Ryswick returned France and England's colonial possessions to their status at the outbreak of King William's War. The years of extreme effort, of terror, peril, and gallantry were, in effect, for nothing. Staking claims to absolute power in North America, neither nation could yet capture and hold the continent. For sixty years each side would marshal its forces, raise armies, build navies and spar intermittently in the West Indies, Acadia in Canada before the issue was finally settled.

Chapter Two

A CORSAIR ON THE BORDER

After decades of relative peace, Catholic persecution of Protestants broke out anew when the militant Louis XIV assumed power in France in 1661. At that time the French town of Bergerac was a great centre of Protestantism in Catholic France, and had suffered terribly during the brutal religious conflict of the Thirty Years War in the first half of the seventeenth century. The town was fought over, taken and retaken by forces of the opposing faiths, its walls, bridges, churches and great houses flattened in the fanatical combat.

Bergerac was now subjected to "dragonnades": royal soldiers were lodged in the homes of Protestant families, with orders to make their stay there as painful and expensive as

possible for the inhabitants. Protestants were encouraged to abjure their faith, under threat of violence or death. Some were condemned to slavery in the King's Mediterranean galleys, others to the verminous lower decks of his sailing navy.

In response, much of the town's population simply migrated downstream to the great port of Bordeaux, from there journeying to the hoped-for liberty of the American colonies. Among them was a young man named Pierre Maisonnat, a boatman with long experience ferrying wines along the Dordogne and Gironde rivers, eager to practice his trade in the new world unhindered by his homeland's incessant strife.

A young Louis XIV, looking bold and martial.

A view of Bordeaux in the eighteenth century: the city grew as France's Atlantic gateway.

Arriving in New France in 1690, he was soon disappointed. French border raids in the winter of 1689, beginning with d'Iberville's assault on Corlaer, had incited terror and sectarian fury in the English colonies. The New England preacher Cotton Mather thundered against the colonies' "enswamped adversaries" haunting the impenetrable woods to the north, and their First Nations allies, referred to spitefully as "Frenchified Pagans." Puritan Boston saw the French raids as blows in a "Spiritual War," fought between the forces of Protestant liberty and Catholic slavery. It was eager to return blow for blow.

New France's easternmost extension was Acadia (Canada's modern-day Maritime provinces). Its capital was Port Royal on the Bay of Fundy. Small and isolated, it was neglected by French authorities and distant from the centre of French power at Quebec. Port Royal was dangerously near New

ASPECT DE TOLLON
DV COTE DE LA GRANDE RADE

Forced service in the verminous lower decks of France's Mediterranean galley fleet was a grim fate awaiting many protestants during the religious wars of the seventeenth century.

Cotton Mather, Massachusetts's fiery preacher of militant Protestantism.

England, however, and ripe for the colonies' retribution.

Providentially, New England's champion soon appeared in the person of Sir William Phips. Tough and boastful, raised in the turbulent Maine borderlands, Phips was wealthy and powerful, having salvaged a fortune coin-by-coin from the flooded hold of a Spanish treasure galleon lying on the rough coral bottom of the Caribbean. Determined to strike the French Catholic threat at its head, Phips prepared expeditions against both Port Royal and Quebec.

So, on May 9, 1690 a force of seven ships and 700 men under Phips' command coasted up the Bay of Fundy, past Goat Island and into the Rivière Dauphin (modern-day Annapolis River), anchoring off a bastioned fort undermined and crumbling in the tide. Behind its rickety walls waited 85 defenders serving 18 decrepit cannon. Among them was the French Protestant exile, Pierre Maisonnat. On the tenth an envoy rowed ashore with an ultimatum: surrender immediately and relinquish all stores and property belonging to the French king. If this was done, private property belonging to the townspeople would be spared. If not, Phips vowed, "By the help of God, on whom alone I trust for assistance, to attack, kill, burn and destroy, and then you may,

Sir William Phips, treasure hunter, self-made man, conqueror of Port Royal.

when too late, wish for that favour which you now refuse."

The defenders of Port Royal did not refuse Phips' favour; in turn, Phips did not respect his terms. The town surrendered, and the New Englanders promptly sacked it. The journal of one participant in the attack makes it clear that nothing, sacred or profane, escaped their greed or fury: "We cut down the cross, rifled the church, pulled down the altar and broke their images ... [we] kept gathering plunder all day." Outraged, the governor of Acadia wrote to demand the return of his personal belongings carried off to Boston: "Six silver spoons, six silver forks, one silver cup in the shape of a gondola, a pair of pistols, three new wigs, a grey vest, four pair of silk garters, two dozen of shirts, six vests of dimity, four night-caps with lace edgings, all my table service of fine tin, all my kitchen linen...." Puritan New England's righteous fury was clearly, in Phips' case at least, mixed with a healthy desire for plunder.

Pierre Maisonnat was carried off to Boston, along with the dimity vests and nightcaps. There he remained for some time after his capture, becoming a subject of King William of England and a member of the town's French Protestant church. The unfamiliar culture, the commercial and spiritual

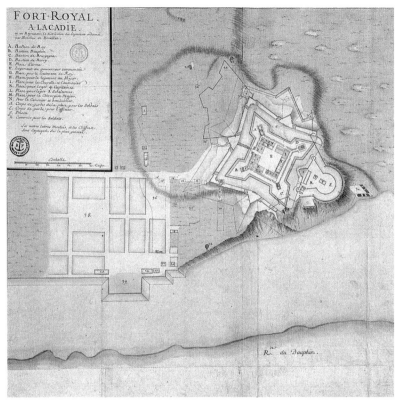

Plan of the French fortifications at Port Royal.

welter of Boston did not, it seems, finally suit him. Sometime between the spring 1690 and the first months of 1692 he again confronted the question of denominational loyalty that had haunted him since his birth in ravaged Bergerac, some 35 years earlier. This time, it seems, he adopted the cause of France's Catholic king, and did so militantly: in January 1692 Maisonnat reappears in the historical record, under the *nom de guerre* "Baptiste," in command of a French privateer and its prize, a rich New England ship.

From 1692 onwards Baptiste sailed in company with other French privateers, provisioning and refitting at Acadian coastal settlements — Port Royal, Minas, Beaubassin (on the site of present day Fort Lawrence) — that were, since Phips' attack, nominally subject to the English crown. But New England forces couldn't control Acadia. In its isolated outposts they would be surrounded by a hostile population, and constantly threatened by native attack on land and privateer attack at sea. As a result, much of the colony remained effectively ungoverned during the war, subject to attacks by New England and West Indian privateers and illicit visits from their French counterparts.

Such French authority as there was in Acadia was

Above: People of the Malecite First Nation near Nashwaak, New Brunswick.
Right: The hard, miserable life of the galeriens.

immediately in harm's way, hunting enemy warships so that he could outfit his small vessel with their captured guns. Impressed with his "intelligence and enterprise," Villebon boasted that if Baptiste did so he would consider signing on with the privateer himself.

The privateer soon justified Villebon's confidence, sailing out of the Saint John River and preying on the busy and dangerous shipping lanes off Boston Harbour. On this, his first cruise, he took eight prizes, including a brigantine loaded with thousands of bushels of desperately needed wheat, captured within sight of the Massachusetts capital. Impressed with Baptiste's initiative and navigational skill, Villebon recommended him as pilot for a major expedition then being planned against targets on the New England coast. The governor outlined the mission to Baptiste and swore him

embodied in Governor Joseph Robinau de Villebon, a diligent and tough-minded former dragoon. Villebon arrived at Port Royal in the summer of 1690, just weeks after Phips had reduced the capital to a ruin. He wisely established his capital in a less exposed location, well up the Saint John River at Nashwaak (opposite modern-day Fredericton), where he was both secure from attack and close to the native allies he relied upon to carry Frontenac's policy of guerrilla warfare to Maine and northern Massachusetts.

Baptiste received a privateering commission from Villebon with a qualified pledge, in view of the privateer's contested loyalties, of "staunch protection, so long as he displayed zeal in the service of his Prince." Baptiste's bold manner soon reassured the governor. He intended to go

to secrecy, but the privateer would keep Villebon's confidence for years before he at last executed the plan.

Baptiste's early successes also won attention from the French court at Versailles, the centre of royal power and influence. He was ordered to report to the Minister of Marine, Louis Phélypeaux de Pontchartrain, who rewarded his captures with command of a small, fast warship, a corvette named the *Bonne*. Departing the great Atlantic port of La Rochelle on April 8, 1694 he soon made the best of his new ship's speed and power. Making landfall at Cape Sable, Nova Scotia in early June, he scattered the New England fishing fleet poaching off the Acadian coast, taking five vessels into the Saint John River and chasing others off the banks.

Baptiste cruised once again to the southward, attacking shipping in Boston's approaches. Fearing his presence there would be revealed, he attacked and sank vessels too small to make worthwhile prizes. On the morning of July 12 he

Seamen were exposed to the rigours of the elements — and of naval discipline — throughout their often short lives.

Louis Phelipeaux de Pontchartrain, French Minister of Marine, responsible for France's American colonies.

captured a ketch loaded with provisions bound for the West Indies. In the afternoon he took a vessel inbound with sugar and molasses, and another out of England with a cargo of cloth and salt. The following day he took a fishing smack and, shorthanded with the need to man so many prizes, set a course back to the Saint John River. En route he met a 44-gun English frigate and lost his first and last prizes. Still, *Bonne* arrived home with ample prizes in tow.

In September 1694 Baptiste was at Minas, refitting before returning south for further prizes. While still at anchor of the Acadian settlement, *Bonne* was struck by a late summer storm, a vicious squall that knocked her over, nearly sinking her. Repairs took until early October, by which time enemy shipping was scarce. In mid-January 1695 he returned to the Saint John River, a prize laden with sugar and molasses in tow, and laid up *Bonne* for the winter after a remarkably effective and profitable privateering season.

In addition to the prizes

the 32-gun English frigate *Sorlings* to windward with a 4-gun brig in consort. Outgunned, with nowhere to run, Baptiste ran his vessel aground broadside to his attackers and fought. Cannon fire raged throughout the morning and afternoon, mangling the English frigate's rigging and fatally crippling *Bonne* by early evening. As darkness fell, Baptiste and his crew salvaged what they could, clambered ashore, and escaped overland through thick swamp and forest to report their misfortune to Villebon.

Baptiste was ordered to return to France and account for the loss of *Bonne* to the Minister of Marine. Departing in the warship *Envieux*, he sojourned in Plaisance while the annual

The French Corsair Dugay-Trouin commanding the fleet against the English. The distinction between privateering and regular naval service was at times fluid, especially in France.

they took, the constant threat posed by French privateers meant New England vessels could no longer fish securely in home waters, much less off the coast of Acadia. Governor Villebon wrote Pontchartrain that Baptiste's attacks kept 400 New Englanders tied up guarding their coasts, and that native frontier attacks kept as many occupied on land.

Soon after privateering resumed the following spring, Baptiste's fortunes turned. Returning from the Massachusetts coast with a fresh prize on the morning of May 24, he sighted

outbound convoy of fishing vessels formed up, embarking briefly on the Saint-Jean-de-Luz privateer *Charmante* for a cruise in the approaches to Boston. *Charmante* took two vessels, including one with eight guns carrying provisions to St. John's, narrowly evading the attentions of English warships in the area.

On his arrival at Versailles, Baptiste reported to Pontchartrain. Any misgivings about the loss of *Bonne* were soon relieved: the Minister of Marine noted that before she

Soleil Royale, *a French ship of the line, from astern.*

was lost he thought the ship too old and decrepit to risk a crew to bring her back to France. Furthermore, she had indeed sunk mere hours after she was captured, taking eight Englishmen with her.

Returning to Acadia in summer 1696, Baptiste at last executed the mission Villebon had outlined to him in secret four years earlier: a combined land and sea attack against frontier strongholds on the New England coast by French and native forces. Months earlier the warships *Envieux* and *Profond* departed the French port of Rochefort under the command of d'Iberville and Simon-Pierre Denys de Bonaventure, stopping en route to take on troops at Quebec and Mi'kmaq fighters at Spanish Harbour, Cape Breton (modern-day Sydney).

Approaching the Saint John River the force encountered two British frigates and a brisk fight followed, in which the 24-gun *Newport* was dismasted and captured, while her sister ship *Sorlings* escaped into the fog. Baptiste piloted the force westward, gathering more soldiers and native fighters along the coast, including 300 men under the legendary commander Jean-Vincent d'Abbadie de Saint-Castin, a French baron linked by marriage to powerful Abenaki families. Saint-Castin was the most influential man on the Acadia-New England frontier, and his presence in the fight was vital.

Their target was Pemaquid, an imposing stone fort east of Maine's Kennebec River. Pemaquid was a vital point on the coast between Boston and Acadia, changing hands several times during King William's War. It was massively rebuilt by William Phips to protect New England's northern frontier and to disrupt Saint-Castin's influence with the Abenaki, the First Nation that "held the northern passes" between New England and New France. In 1696 the fort was defended by 95 militiamen serving 15 cannon, and was provisioned for a siege.

The attacking force arrived on August 13 and promptly disembarked troops and guns. As native sharpshooters took up positions commanding the ramparts, cannon and mortar were prepared for bombardment. Saint-Castin sent a letter to the fort's commander, Pascho Chubb, demanding surrender and threatening no mercy if the garrison insisted on holding

Fort Pemaquid, New England's northern bastion on the Maine coast.

out. Chubb boldly replied that he would fight on, "even if the sea were covered with French ships and the land with Indians."

The French responded by lobbing explosive shells into the fort. Outnumbered and surrounded the defenders soon realized the impossibility of their situation and surrendered. Entering the fort the attackers found a captive Abenaki fighter in chains, terribly abused, so d'Iberville confined the disarmed garrison to a nearby island to spare them the warriors' vengeance. His forces then systematically dismantled New England's northern bastion stone by stone before sailing against English settlements serving the rich fisheries of Newfoundland. It was a task that d'Iberville executed with terrible completeness.

Within weeks of the attack on Pemaquid, New England struck back at the centre of French power in Acadia: Fort Saint-Joseph, at Nashwaak. This, Villebon's capital, was where he directed native attacks by land and privateers' by sea. In early October 1696 two frigates and four smaller vessels carrying a force of several hundred New England militia and native allies appeared off the mouth of the Saint John River. Villebon rallied the meagre forces he had, denouncing the attacking "rascals" and reminding his men that they were fighting "to sustain in this country the honour of the service of the greatest King in the world." Baptiste, eager to serve his sovereign, soon arrived from his home

"Homme Acadien": a European view of a Mi'kmaq hunter. The Mi'kmaq First Nation were staunch allies of France in its long contest with England.

nearby and took up an exposed position in the most vulnerable part of the fort.

The fort's dogs barked incessantly through the night of 17 October. As the priest said Mass the next morning, Villebon saw boatloads of enemy soldiers arrive before the fort. Manning the ramparts, he allowed the attackers to advance within range of the fort's guns before opening fire and forcing them to retreat. The New Englanders disembarked and dug hasty trenches facing the fort, arming them with small cannon. Baptiste and his men took up positions directly opposite, firing constantly on the exposed guns until nightfall, effectively keeping them out of action. When the New Englanders tried to light fires in the darkness the fort's gunners replied with volleys of grapeshot.

After a cold, sleepless night the attackers' position was made even worse, as Villebon concentrated his artillery fire on their cannon, destroying one gun and keeping the others out of action. Musket fire continued throughout the day. By evening the attackers' camp was ablaze and the French could hear them loading their boats for a retreat. Baptiste harried the retreating militia with relentless musket fire. Villebon was convinced that if more fighters had joined him, the New Englanders would have been completely routed.

Baptiste salvaged two flat-bottomed boats, pirogues, abandoned during the disorderly retreat. Later he used these vessels to transport soldiers wounded in the fight to Minas.

There he outfitted them for privateering, raising crews among the settlement's young men.

Freed from the threat of imminent attack, Acadia's defenders nevertheless faced an especially harsh winter. In February Baptiste arrived off the mouth of the Saint John River, having battled Fundy's contrary currents and choppy seas for 58 days on the 150-kilometre passage from Minas. Too weak from the ordeal to ascend the river to Nashwaak himself, he sent a message to Villebon requesting a commission for a new

A view of mercantile establishments, Boston, as they appeared late in the century.

privateering cruise. The governor encouraged him to continue fighting zealously, to attack and burn coastal settlements, showing mercy to women and children only.

By the first week of March the privateers were on the point of starvation, living on nothing but shellfish they gathered close inshore. In desperate need of provisions, they found eight fishing vessels at anchor in Casco Bay and decided to attack despite the discouraging odds. When night fell they boarded two vessels and subdued their crews, the sounds of the struggle waking others in the anchorage. Two vessels slipped their cables and escaped. Pitched battles erupted on the dark, swaying decks of the remaining four. Baptiste's men subdued the fishing crews with difficulty, killing seven, wounding four others and taking twenty prisoners. Baptiste himself was wounded three times and many among his crew were likewise injured.

Still suffering from his wounds, Baptiste transferred his crew from the pirogues to the captured fishing vessels. Sending his prisoners ashore, he prepared to continue his cruise when two privateers out of Salem, Massachusetts, surprised him before he could get underway. Once within range, Baptiste's crew fired on the Salem vessels, forcing them to retreat. When they returned the next day Baptiste's men again engaged them sharply, killing four and forcing them to break off their attack. This time, one of the Salem vessels stayed at the mouth of the harbour while the other sailed to summon help. His crews weakened by prolonged hunger and repeated combat, Baptiste escaped on an ebbing tide, sailing for Minas to reprovision and refit his hard-won prizes.

In May 1697 Baptiste's fortune again changed for the worse. Captured at last off the New England coast he was cast into a bare Boston prison cell where he was treated especially harshly, due perhaps to his notoriously successful attacks on the colonies' fisheries. The end of the war did not immediately mitigate the harsh treatment. While Boston learned of the Treaty of Ryswick, in December, Baptiste remained in captivity until the following summer. Once released, he did not long remain free.

The terms of the treaty at last excluded English fishers from the coasts of Acadia, and Baptiste was charged with enforcing this exclusion. As he attempted to do so, in 1702, New Englanders captured and charged him with piracy, disputing the legitimacy of his zealous enforcement of French interest in peacetime. Many in Boston called for his execution. Baptiste was held in a dank Boston fort for four years as diplomatic correspondence passed between Boston and Quebec: the French governor making high-level prisoner exchanges contingent on Baptiste's release; the English governor accusing the privateer of "lowness" and "cowardice," calling him a "rascal" and a "rogue." Finally, in 1706, Baptiste was released in exchange for the prominent minister John Williams, who had been carried to Canada in the devastating February, 1704 raid on Deerfield, Massachusetts, in the course of yet another frontier war.

True to the pledge he made to Governor Villebon years

Medal struck by France in 1720 to commemorate the founding of its new American strongpoint, Louisbourg.

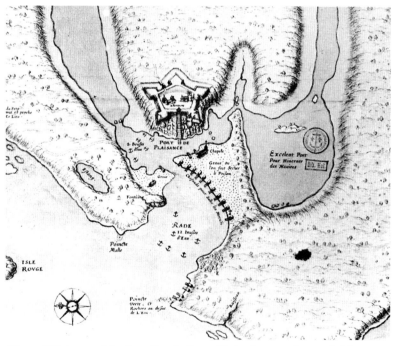

Plan of Plaisance, Newfoundland. Its ample harbour and ease of defense made it an ideal resort for French privateers.

earlier, Baptiste remained resolute in the service of his Prince during his final years. After his release in 1706 he was appointed port captain at the Acadian settlement of Beaubassin, responsible for navigation in the head of the Bay of Fundy. In 1709 and 1711 he returned to Plaisance, preying on English shipping working the great offshore fishing banks of Newfoundland.

Baptiste's final appearance in history followed France's loss of Acadia and Plaisance in 1713's Treaty of Utrecht. The French government, recognizing his immense knowledge of the North Atlantic coasts, consulted him on the site for its new settlement on Cape Breton Island. That settlement — named Louisbourg in honour of the French Catholic sovereign — was itself destined to become a famous privateering port, and an unbearable threat to the interests of England in America.

Chapter Three

BARON OF THE WILDERNESS

T he brilliantly successful assault on Fort Pemaquid in
the summer of 1696 was the most concentrated
exercise of French power in North America in the
entire course of King William's War.
Pemaquid was a crucial target, the
easternmost anchor of New England's
northern frontier defences and a
strongpoint interrupting French trade and
military relations with their First Nations
allies.

Frontenac's raids, Phips' expeditions,
years of back-and-forth naval and
privateering warfare along the North
Atlantic coast all highlighted the vital
need to control the frontier between
France and England's American colonies.
And as the attacks on Lachine, Corlaer and
Pemaquid vividly demonstrated, control of
the borderlands depended in large
measure on the favour of the First Nations
people who inhabited them. That favour,

in turn, depended on the skill and diplomacy of a few chosen
commanders on either side.

When war resumed in North America in 1702 — Queen
Anne's War — both sides appreciated the vital
need to secure the borderlands from enemy
attack. Massachusetts renewed its efforts to win
the allegiance or neutrality of native peoples
on the frontier —Abenaki, Malecite and
Mi'kmaq — disrupting communications with
the French, opening rival trade relations, and
aiming to rebuild the ruin of Pemaquid.
France, weakened and impoverished by
decades of Louis XIV's relentless campaigning,
was forced to rely on the boldness and
ingenuity of its commanders and soldiers in
America. Before 1697 the boldest and most
ingenious man on the frontier was Jean-
Vincent d'Abaddie, third baron Saint-Castin,

*A fanciful nineteenth-century portrait of Baron Saint-
Castin, père.*

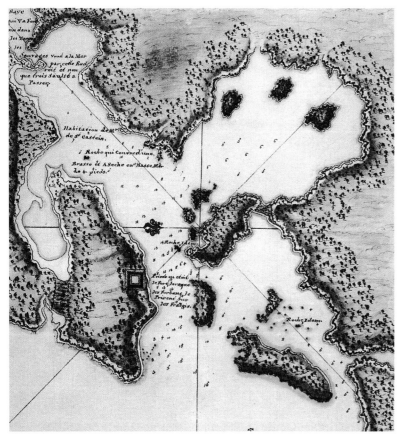

Above: Plan of the harbour at Pentagouet, France's strongpoint on the Maine coast and long-time home of the Saint-Castin family.
Right: Engraving of the site of Abenaki mission, Kennebec.

sovereignty and allegiance on the disputed Acadian frontier. His home on the Penobscot River at Pentagouet (modern-day Castine, Maine) marked the border between French and English for many years. It was sacked repeatedly: by Dutch privateers in 1674 and 1676, by Salem fishers in 1682 and by New York Governor Edmund Andros in 1688. Saint-Castin was closely integrated into the culture of the local First Nations. He married Pidianske, daughter of Madockawando, a powerful Abenaki leader, and lived for three decades with the native people of the region. His unique attributes made him the fulcrum on which the frontier turned, and both French and English wooed or coerced him as necessary. When the third baron returned to France in 1702, never to return, the fate of the frontier hung in the balance.

So, as New England moved to secure its frontiers with the renewal of war, France's position in western Acadia became increasingly precarious. Acadian governor Joseph Monbeton de Brouillan was painfully aware of his capital's dangerous proximity to Boston and tried to adopt a position of neutrality, only to see it shattered by aggressive attacks from the sea. In the autumn of 1702 Massachusetts' privateers sailed unopposed against French shipping in the western

commander of Abenaki forces at the Pemaquid victory. Saint-Castin was seen in New England as the *éminence grise* behind horrific massacres at the settlements of Piscataqua, Casco, Exeter, Oyster River and Kittery, all mauled by lightning raids in King William's War.

Saint-Castin's life exactly mirrored the shifts of

Atlantic, the Gulf of St. Lawrence and the Bay of Fundy. By mid-September they had taken at least 14 French vessels, most on the coasts of Acadia and in the approaches to its restored capital, Port Royal. The French colony's fishery was effectively wiped out. By winter, privateering attacks assumed the status of a blockade, intercepting stores and provisions bound for Acadia's small garrison and, most crucially, for its native allies poised on the northern frontier of New England.

Mindful of Port Royal's fate in 1690, de Brouillan reluctantly adopted the aggressive policy of his predecessors and worked to rebuild the town's capacity to strike back at New England interests. Once again, France needed bold and ingenious men in America. Governor de Brouillan soon found one in the person of Bernard-Anselme, son of Jean-Vincent d'Abbadie, third baron of Saint-Castin and Pidianske. Saint-Castin *fils* was born at Pentagouet in 1689, the year his father attacked Pemaquid — then a primitive outpost on the Maine coast — for the first time.

Raised by his maternal relatives and trained in warfare by his father, he was a 15-year-old boy studying at Quebec's seminary when called upon to lead Acadian fighters and their First Nations allies. Supported and directed by Acadian governor de Brouillan and then by his aggressive successor, Daniel

Benjamin Church led New England forces against Acadia, destroying the settlement of Beaubassin.

d'Auger de Subercase, Bernard-Anselme demonstrated his ancestral talent for arms and diplomacy, growing ever more closely linked to the town and to its small, committed community of warriors.

In 1704, New England forces attacked the French and their allies in the borderlands of the Penobscot River and then struck the Acadian heartland itself. They burned the settlements of Minas and Beaubassin, destroying dykelands, crops and livestock, getting wildly drunk from looted cellars and hauling plunder and prisoners back to Boston. But Port Royal — "a nest of hornets provoked to fly out upon us," in Cotton Mather's resonant words — remained untouched. It continued to send out privateers and continued to support its First Nations allies in the borderlands. Port Royal would have to be destroyed, as it had been again and again in the preceding decades.

On June 6 a New England force of 1100 soldiers and 250 sailors arrived off the town with a

A view from the fort at Annapolis Royal (French Port Royal), looking southward—the direction from which came repeated attacks in the seventeenth and eighteenth centuries.

French cannon at the fort, Annapolis Royal.

fleet of 24 vessels. Prominent among the town's 400 defenders, Saint-Castin acted to assume his father's place in the defence of New France. The attacking troops disembarked the same day and began their advance, and were soon met with fierce resistance from the outnumbered garrison, striking repeatedly from the woods surrounding the fort. The attackers established a beachhead only with great difficulty and in the face of constant French sallies. In one attack, Acadia's new governor, Subercase himself, had his horse shot from under him.

On June 16 the New Englanders attempted to storm the defences, but their frontal assault was driven back by the fort's artillery. Simultaneously, Saint-Castin led a party of three dozen Acadians and Abenaki out of the town, attacking enemy soldiers who were burning houses and killing livestock. An intense fight resulted, in which Saint-Castin himself killed 10 men. Repeatedly thwarted despite their superior numbers, the dispirited New Englanders re-embarked and departed for Boston the next day.

Port Royal survived, but was terribly weakened: the retreating force had destroyed every structure, animal and crop for miles around. When Pierre Morpain arrived in the port in mid-August, trailing prizes laden with provisions, he was greeted as a saviour, but the jubilation was short-lived. The New Englanders returned on August 20, their forces augmented by another 600 fresh troops. Again they landed and set up positions opposite the fort. Again Subercase dispatched war parties and loosed artillery fire from the ramparts, driving the attackers back towards the river.

Saint-Castin and his party of 60 Abenaki intercepted their retreat, harrying the superior force with relentless musketry. The governor marched out with a force of 250 men to stake an advance defensive position, again forcing the enemy back. Saint-Castin and his fighters fell upon the hard-pressed New

Englanders and vicious close combat ensued, a wild melee of sword thrusts, rifle-butts and axe-blows. Fifteen French defenders, including Saint-Castin himself, were injured, and one young soldier died from his wounds. The New Englanders suffered much higher casualties, losing more than 100 men. The attackers remained before Port Royal, paralyzed, for three more days, finally raising anchor on August 24. The twice-failed expedition was greeted with derision on its return to Boston, the townspeople mocking the defeated militiamen with chamber pots and wooden swords.

Despite the New Englanders' defeat, life did not soon improve for the population of Port Royal. The countryside had been ruined. France, on the verge of ruin herself, had virtually ceased to supply the colony. Governor Subercase worked diligently to improve the condition of Acadia, going so far as to give his bed-linens to the poor and sell his belongings to repair the fort's breached walls. Most significantly, however, he gave unstinting support for the small, closely-knit navy of privateers operating out of the town. Among the most prominent was the town's gallant defender, Bernard-Anselme, now fourth baron of Saint-Castin after his father's 1707 death. That same year he married Marie-Charlotte d'Amours de Chauffours, sister-in-law of the famous privateer Pierre Morpain, further strengthening his ties to Port Royal and its martial elite.

Saint-Castin outfitted a privateer for the 1709 season and sailed against the shipping of New England, adapting his boldness and talent for guerrilla attack to sea fighting. By this time in the war privateering, like the incessant raiding in the borderlands, had become as much an attack on the enemy's psychological well-being as on its commercial or military interests. Some prizes — small fishing vessels especially — were without practical value and could not be profitably sold

As Louis XIV's wars dragged on, France became increasingly destitute as depicted in this period painting.

Musket fragment from a contemporary New England shipwreck: Elizabeth and Mary, *part of Phips' failed expedition against Quebec.*

or ransomed. But quick, violent descents on enemy vessels peacefully pursuing their business in home waters served much the same purpose as hit-and-run frontier attacks: they terrorized the enemy population, making them reluctant to undertake everyday activities. French privateers, Abenaki and Mi'kmaq fighters alike preyed on unsuspecting fishers, peacefully at anchor in isolated coves, throughout the long wars of New France and New England.

Port Royal privateers took large, rich prizes as well. In 1709 alone, Saint-Castin and the privateers of Port Royal — Pierre Morpain, Baptiste and Louis Denys de la Ronde — took 35 vessels and nearly 500 prisoners. Inevitably, this led to renewed calls in Boston that the "hornets' nest" be taken and

destroyed once and for all. Port Royal's days as a privateering port were numbered.

The following year the English returned to the town, arriving in October with an expedition of 2000 New England militia and regular soldiers, supported by a fleet of 36 vessels, including seven warships. This time the force came prepared for a siege. It soon unloaded its artillery and began bombarding the town. Governor Subercase, with only 250 dispirited defenders under his command, could do nothing. The town capitulated on October 13. As Subercase marched out of the conquered fort, he expressed his bold hope that the opposing commanders would meet in battle once more — and soon.

Saint-Castin was at sea when the besieging force arrived, but his ketch was taken soon after in Passamaquoddy Bay. He managed to escape overland with his crew, returning to find

Plaisance later in the eighteenth century.

the town firmly in enemy hands. The English, mindful of Saint-Castin's influence with First Nations fighters (as they had been of his father's), treated him with considerable respect, hoping to entice him to their side. They failed. After carrying news of Port Royal's fall overland through the forest to Quebec, he journeyed to his ancestral home at Pentagouet on the Maine frontier, where he recruited a guerrilla force of 40 Abenaki fighters. Returning to Port Royal in June 1711, the force assaulted a party from the English garrison, killing 20 men and wounding many others.

Convinced by this experience in occupied Acadia that Port Royal could be retaken, he worked to organize a besieging force. A modest expedition of 200 men and a dozen officers formed up, and Pierre Morpain was dispatched from the Newfoundland settlement of Plaisance to provision it. But reports of a large Royal Navy force then marshalling in Boston ended Saint-Castin's hopes for an attack. Later, corsairs from the famed French privateering port of St. Malo schemed to retake the town. Nevertheless, Port Royal would never again fly a French flag.

When his hopes of retaking Port Royal failed, Saint-Castin returned to his home on the Acadia-New England frontier, using his influence to maintain France's alliance with the Abenaki. Instructed to reassure his First Nations kinsmen that their security depended on maintaining the Catholic religion and to urge them to continue attacking the English, Saint-Castin distributed vital war materials to the Abenaki: muskets, powder, shot and blankets. But when the supplies from France ceased to arrive, the Abenaki ceased to listen to French promises, no matter how familiar and persuasive their envoy. Saint-Castin soon reported to his superiors that English merchants and missionaries were

Portrait of France's great corsair, Jean Bart of Dunkerque. At this time France's corsairs undertook elaborate expeditions usually associated with national navies.

The walled port of St. Malo was one of France's great centres of privateering. In the days after Port Royal's fall, St. Malo privateers plotted to retake the town.

received favourably in Abenaki communities. The Acadia-New England borderlands were lost.

When Queen Anne's War ended in 1713, the Acadian mainland was transferred to English control and the frontier shifted northward, to Île Royale (modern-day Cape Breton). Canso and Port Toulouse replaced Pentagouet and Pemaquid as the outposts of empire. France's Minister of Marine requested Saint-Castin do all he could to convince the Abenaki to move to the new base. He made every effort, but they would not move. Saint-Castin himself declined the

opportunity to build a new home in the wilds of Île Royale, moving instead to France to reclaim the baronial estate that bore his name but which he had never yet seen. For the rest of his life, until his early death in 1720, he fought in the French courts to establish his title against usurpers who questioned the legitimacy of his claims. He failed after repeated attempts. After a lifetime combating English fighters in the wild borderlands of America, he was defeated by the machinations of the lawyers of France.

Chapter Four

THE ANCIENT WARRIOR

The settlements of the Acadian heartland were hard-pressed by the summer of 1707. New England forces sacked Beaubassin (modern-day Fort Lawrence) and Minas in 1704. In June 1707 Port Royal suffered a joint attack of English and colonial forces, and would suffer another in August. The first attack left the town devastated: its houses burned, orchards cut down, crops uprooted and livestock slaughtered. Weakened by hunger and anxiety, the population kept watch on the river, waiting for another expedition to appear. In the second week of August sails rose on the horizon. Many in the town feared the worst.

A view of Annapolis Royal showing its fortifications.

The ships coasting up the Rivière Dauphin (today's Annapolis River) to Port Royal on August 12, 1707, however, carried a providential gift. A privateer from the French West Indian colony of Saint-Domingue soon anchored off the fort, with two prizes in tow. One was laden with much-needed provisions, including 750 barrels of flour, 25 casks of butter, and large quantities of ham and lard to replenish the town's badly depleted food stores. When New England forces did return eight days later, Port Royal's population was well fed and its garrison supplemented by the privateer's crew, who fought courageously to repel the

captain of a privateer vessel himself, *Intrépide*, taking his first prize into Cuba in 1707. The same year he cruised northward along the coast of New England, taking the two prizes he brought to Port Royal that August day: a slaving vessel and a merchant ship.

With the latest assault on Port Royal deflected and the town reprovisioned, Morpain left Acadia in late September, taking with him a young man named Robert Chevalier (also known as de Beauchêne), who had decided to begin an apprentice-ship in the privateer's art. Expecting a coarse and violent life aboard the private man-of-war, Beauchêne was stunned to find Morpain conducting morning and evening prayer on his

Above: The highly lucrative, slave-driven sugar industry was the engine that drove France's West Indian expansion.
Right: Saint-Domingue was a sought-after prize in the European scramble for West Indian colonies. In the early eighteenth century it was in French hands and hosted a growing population of privateers – including Pierre Morpain.

invaders. Acadia's energetic and hardheaded governor, Daniel d'Auger de Subercase, saw the privateers' arrival as a miraculous intervention of France's guardian spirit. He worked hard to keep them in Port Royal, paying special attention to their captain, Pierre Morpain.

Morpain was born in the ancient fortified town of Blaye, downriver from Bordeaux on the Gironde, in 1686. He went to sea at the age of 17, sailing in merchant ships and then, from 1706, in privateers out of the West Indian colony of Saint-Domingue (now the Dominican Republic). He was soon cruise. Once in the West Indies, Beauchêne would undoubtedly observe that Morpain was not typical of Saint-Domingue privateers.

Saint-Domingue in the early seventeenth century was notorious for the free-living manner of its inhabitants, a "Republic of Adventurers." Privateering thrived in the island colony: subject to attack from all sides, privateers were vital to its defence; furthermore, its government officials personally bankrolled privateers' cruises and profited from their captures. Traditionally the Saint-Domingue privateers, or *flibustiers*, were a breed apart, as much gunmen as they were sailors. They preferred vessels of the simplest rig, and were more adept at handling pistols than handling sail.

They were as likely to hit targets on land as at sea, the "descent" — the capture and ransom of coastal settlements and their inhabitants — being a typical action. At sea they sought the most vulnerable prizes, and were not always scrupulous about the nationality of those they attacked. The English buccaneer William Dampier called West Indian privateering a "loose roving way of life," and marine historian J.S. Bromley lists its practitioners' characteristics as "self-will, caprice, dislike of work...disordered and unwashed clothing, their habit of singing while companions tried to sleep and shooting to make a noise...their blasphemies and debaucheries."

In contrast, Morpain was a bold and disciplined seaman. After his return from Acadia in the autumn of 1707 he didn't

Naval operations in Dominican waters.

A typical—and terrifying—tactic of West Indian privateers was the armed descent on unsuspecting coastal towns.

shrink from engaging big, dangerous prizes, taking a large Dutch vessel that he outfitted as a privateer, and overcoming a 24-gun frigate with a crew of more than 100 men.

In 1709 Morpain returned to Acadia as captain of *Marquis de Choiseul-Beaupré*, and was greeted as a hero by the grateful inhabitants. Governor Subercase provided him with local pilots and Morpain used them well. In the course of a 10-day cruise he took nine prizes and sank a further four that refused to yield. He escaped a sharp encounter with a Massachusetts coast guard vessel, killing her captain in the encounter and gaining a prominent place in New England folklore. Morpain remained in Acadian waters for two tense months that summer, awaiting a renewed New England attack that most felt to be imminent. When, late in the season, the expected attack hadn't come, Morpain returned to Saint-Domingue. Not, however, before making his growing connection to Acadia permanent, marrying Marie-Josèphe d'Amours de Chauffours, sister-in-law of Bernard-Anselme d'Abbadie de Saint-Castin.

Port Royal was attacked by New England forces for the last time in the autumn of 1710, the town finally capitulating in October. Morpain was at sea when it fell, and soon relocated with Marie-Josèphe to Plaisance, which remained in French control. Subercase had formerly governed this

A French flibustiers *boarding a Spanish Galleon. West Indian* flibustiers *often used the simplest vessels and tactics in their attacks.*

fortified Newfoundland town, working with his usual energy to develop a base for privateers attacking the island's English fisheries. He attracted Canadian and French fighters — from St. Malo, Saint Jean de Luz, Bordeaux, Granville — and, increasingly after the loss of Port Royal, Acadian and Mi'kmaq fighters as well. In the course of the war these men captured dozens of enemy ships.

At Plaisance, French authorities learned of Saint-Castin's plans to attack English-occupied Port Royal with the native fighters he commanded. Morpain was given the task of carrying guns, ammunition, blankets and other supplies to Acadia in support of the insurgency. Setting out, he soon encountered a well-armed enemy vessel and engaged it, the encounter continuing until Morpain was cast overboard by the violence of the action. He was captured and taken to St. John's, but was soon exchanged and returned to Plaisance with testimonies from the English authorities praising his skill and courage.

In the last days of Queen Anne's War he cruised southward again, taking a large Dutch prize into Saint-Domingue. It was Morpain's last warlike act for a very long time. For five years he had preyed on the shipping of the English and Dutch West Indies, of New England and Newfoundland, earning an almost mythical reputation among his enemies as "Morepang the Pirate." With the

Silver coffee service from Louisbourg. The town prospered in the peaceful interlude leading up to the 1745 siege.

coming of peace in 1713, he and Marie-Josèphe returned to his French birthplace, Blaye, but by 1715, he was back in America serving his king. Appointed port captain to the new settlement of Île Royale (Cape Breton), he oversaw the establishment of a fishing village that grew to be the great commercial centre and fortress of Louisbourg.

As port captain, Morpain was an important citizen in the developing colony, surveying Île Royale's treacherous approaches, overseeing improvements to the port, acting as coastal pilot, teaching navigation and engaging in trade. Over the next ten years his career reflected the ups and downs of life in a rough and busy town: in 1717 controversy erupted when he was accused of losing his nerve on a passage in a North Atlantic storm; in 1718 he fought a duel; and in 1721 he was promoted to the rank of *capitaine de flûte*.

Then, on August 27, 1725, Louisbourg awoke to news of a terrible shipwreck near the hamlet of Baleine, a few miles north of the town. The royal flute *Chameau*, 44 guns, carrying officials and payroll for the Canadian administration from France to Quebec, had encountered a powerful southeast gale the day before. The ship was driven before the storm at unmanageable speed, striking an offshore reef and disintegrating with a force that scattered bodies and debris over a wide swath of sea floor. All 316 souls aboard perished in the night, drowned below decks or pounded to death against the rocky shore.

When officials from Louisbourg arrived the next morning — Morpain almost certainly among them — the beaches were strewn with a grisly tangle of splintered timbers, glinting coin and bodies. A Recollet priest from the town, Père Michel-Ange LeDuff, spent a week overseeing the collection and burial of 180 victims in a common grave at the site. The rest were never recovered.

This terrible duty completed, officials turned to

Modern-day re-enactors stand guard at Dauphin Gate, Fortress Louisbourg.

recovery of the cannon and treasure embarked on *Chameau.* As port captain, Morpain was responsible for salvage efforts, receiving in return one-third of all goods recovered. The divers he hired in Quebec arrived too late in the season to start work in 1725. The following summer Morpain's salvage vessel was stolen, causing further delays; rumours held that the ship was taken at the instigation of a New England fishing captain then visiting Louisbourg. In September his men searched for the wreck's hull, dragging the bottom with grappling hooks and diving in the dark, frigid water, protected from the cold by a thin layer of grease and a diet of fresh meat and chocolate. In December salvage efforts ended in disappointment. Morpain had located none of the ship's guns and only a fraction of her treasure. Salvage from the shoreline provided a very modest profit.

His wife, Marie-Josèphe, died at Louisbourg in 1726, and the following decades passed quietly for Morpain. When

A view of Louisbourg, harbour and town, in 1731.

King George's War broke on North America in 1744, the old privateer returned to his trade with undiminished skill and ardour, at the advanced age of 58. Louisbourg learned of the outbreak a full month before Boston, in early May 1744, giving its privateers the advantage of surprise. Privateering out of the port started in late May with attacks on New England fishing vessels working the offshore banks. By the end of June the waters off Louisbourg were, for the moment, free of enemy shipping.

Morpain assumed command of the colony's coast guard, the schooner *Succès,* and her crew of 106 men. The ship was armed and outfitted with the town's best provisions — Bordeaux wines, imported cheese, fresh meat — and medicines for her cruises off the coast of Île Royale, in search of enemy warships and prizes. In the second week of July *Succès* took two vessels, *Nancy* and *Kingsbury,* bringing them into Louisbourg in triumph. By the end of the month Morpain took command of the 52-gun naval vessel *Caribou,* recently arrived from Quebec, using her to retake a French prize and then to capture an English schooner off the coast of Newfoundland.

Morpain's effect on the wartime psychology of New England may have been even greater than the damage he inflicted on its shipping. The occupying garrison at Nova Scotia's Annapolis Royal quaked at false rumours that he was approaching with a force of 500 fighters. In the summer of 1744, visitors recorded extreme anxiety in the English colonies at the success of French privateers. In one confused encounter off Connecticut, English vessels mistakenly engaged one another, convinced that "old Morepang, the French rover, who in former times used to plunder these parts" was attacking them.

Later in the season, New England privateers mounted a counter-offensive against Île Royale, repeatedly identifying the enemy they encountered as Morpain — whether he was actually present or not. Captain Samuel Waterhouse of

Boston took French prizes off Cape Breton in the privateer *Hawk* before being chased away from the coast in September by "a privateer schooner commanded by the famous French Captain Morepang and by two ships."

In late September the Boston privateer *Ranger* under a Captain Richardson reported a sharp encounter in a snow squall, against a 14-gun vessel he assumed was commanded by Morpain. Closing with the French vessel, Richardson opened up simultaneously with his cannon, swivel guns and muskets, damaging the enemy's stern. A fierce battle followed in heavy seas and at close quarters. *Ranger* suffered two dead, including the helmsman, killed at the ship's wheel. Nine were wounded, including Richardson himself, shot through the leg but defiantly on deck throughout the fight. Seas breaking over the ships washed the dead into the ocean. Finally the French vessel crippled *Ranger*'s sails and got to windward, escaping the deeply laden New England vessel. When someone later advanced the conjecture that "Morepang" was in fact an Irishman named Murphy, Richardson replied, "Let him be who he will, he fought very courageously. He ran fore and aft with his cutlass driving about his people and a great number of marines."

The winter of 1744-45 was an especially hard one at

The launch of a French ship. France's navy was Europe's finest through much of the 18th century. Relatively little of it was devoted to the protection of New France, as the defenders of Louisbourg well knew.

Louisbourg. The town's survival depended on its warships and privateers keeping sea lanes open to vital provisions — a task again assisted by Morpain, who cruised the Gulf of St. Lawrence in company with a St. Malo privateer. The deprived garrison mutinied over the winter. As spring approached, townspeople watched the horizon with anxiety and trepidation, waiting for the enemy to reappear.

Their worst fears were soon realized. On May 11 an expedition of 3000 New England militiamen, supported by four warships, each mounting at least 40 guns, appeared in Gabarus Bay, a few miles southwest of the fortress. The inexperienced militia immediately began a bold, daylight landing, pouring troops and material ashore. The officers in command at Louisbourg, young and untried in combat, seemed unable to take decisions to check the advance. Two of the oldest and most seasoned fighters in the fortress — Antoine Le Poupet de la Boularderie and Pierre Morpain — saw the folly of giving the New Englanders a beachhead within sight of the town, and demanded immediate counter-offensive action.

Boularderie maintained the attackers were still wet, afraid and disoriented. They would not be so for long. He demanded soldiers with which to attack the landing, but the fortress's commanders gave him a mere two dozen. By the time Boularderie and Morpain left the fortress walls, 1500 New Englanders had landed. Boularderie immediately realized Louisbourg's officers had waited too long and told Morpain their sortie was futile. The privateer replied, "It doesn't matter. Let's march." As the tiny force advanced through the woods, landing-ships close inshore spotted them and brought their cannon to bear. Morpain ordered the thinning line of soldiers — perhaps a dozen remaining at this time — to spread out, presenting a harder target for the gunners.

Forest and waterfront at Annapolis Royal, from the Atlantic Neptune, by J.F.W. Desbarres.

It was soon clear that a gallant advance had become a foolish one. Boularderie pleaded for immediate, orderly retreat, warning Morpain that he "knew nothing of fighting on land, as I know nothing of the sea." Heedless, Morpain kept advancing and the force was soon surrounded. Despairing, Boularderie shouted, "The place where we stand is our tomb!" For most of the French soldiers present, it soon was. Savage combat followed: seven of the remaining twelve soldiers were killed, the other five wounded. Boularderie himself was shot twice and taken prisoner. Morpain was dragged from the field and hidden by a slave who accompanied him into battle. Days later they managed to return to the fortress.

By then Louisbourg was surrounded by a New England force whose landing had been opposed by the old fighters'

mad sally alone. In the course of the siege Morpain assumed responsibility for the fortress's seaward defence. He worked tirelessly and without sleep, commanding militia units, directing artillery, constructing batteries to strengthen weak points and encouraging the defenders. To no avail. On June 28, New England troops marched into the town, victorious. Morpain was as magnanimous in defeat as he was courageous in the fight, stating that before the siege he thought the New England men were cowards, but now he thought if they had a pick-ax and spade "they could dig their way to hell and storm it."

The old warrior had lost the battle, but France had not yet lost the war. Soon after Louisbourg's surrender Morpain returned again to Blaye to recover from the two years' campaigning. He then joined one last American fight, at Île Dauphine, Mobile Bay, Louisiana, in 1748. In October, King George's War ended with the signing of the Treaty of Aix-la-Chapelle. The outcome of the contest between France and England in America was once again merely postponed: a few years later the struggle would again break out, this time to be carried to its conclusion. Unfortunately for France, Pierre Morpain would not be there at the end. He died at Rochefort on August 21, 1749, still in command of a royal ship.

Chapter Five

A PRIVATEER'S MISFORTUNE

Canso's bleak harbour has sheltered Europeans — drawn by its unrivalled proximity to offshore fishing banks — from 1504 or even earlier. Control of the port shifted repeatedly over the centuries, but from 1713 it was English, a counterpoise to the French presence in Île Royale. Its role in the fishery shrank as Newfoundland's rose, but its strategic importance remained. In 1744 Canso was garrisoned by English troops and protected by an English warship, HMS *Kinsale*. It was a crucial and effective base for intercepting illicit trade between

The reconstructed Louisbourg waterfront: its calm belies the town's contentious past.

Dutch 'East Indiamen' ride comfortably in gusty winds and choppy seas. 'East Indiamen' were large, heavily-built ships designed to carry rich cargoes on long passages.

the French fortress at Louisbourg and the rich agricultural heartland of Acadia, now renamed Nova Scotia and under increasingly firm English control.

Canso's success as a spoiler of French ambitions on Île Royale was apparent in Louisbourg in the winter of 1743-44. The preceding fishing season was the worst on record. The fortress's 3000 inhabitants suffered terribly from food shortages. As spring approached, the town's poor subsisted on mussels and winkles gathered on the shore, and guards were posted to protect the storehouses. So, when a small vessel out of St. Malo made port on May 3, 1744, many in Louisbourg were elated to learn that a state of war existed yet again between France and England. At last they could strike the enemy who

was blocking trade with their cousins in Acadia. Perhaps, with luck and support from France, they could retake settlements lost thirty years earlier: Beaubassin, Minas and Port Royal.

The ship carried letters from the French Minister of Marine, Jean Frédéric Phélypeaux de Maurepas, urging Louisbourg's inhabitants to strike enemy fisheries and shipping along the coast and to strike quickly, exploiting the advantage of surprise. He included blank privateering commissions for the commandant of Île Royale, Jean Baptiste Louis le Prévost du Quesnel, to distribute at will. Reading further, du Quesnel found startling and dispiriting news: six ships of the *Compagnie des Indes* — inbound to France from the Cape of Good Hope with rich cargoes of tea, coffee, porcelain, spices — had been diverted to Louisbourg to await naval escort. By July the town would have to feed another 700 men, many desperately ill after months at sea. Suddenly, the need to dislodge the English from their nest at Canso became urgent.

Three weeks after Louisbourg learned of the war an expedition left to assault the English port, under the command of Joseph Dupont du Vivier, captain of the *Compagnies Franches de la Marine*. On May 23, 350 French soldiers, Swiss mercenaries and local fishers coasted southward in a miscellany of battered boats, shepherded and protected by two privateers commanded by the first recipients of du Quesnel's commissions: the veteran fighter Pierre Morpain, and an obscure fisher named Joannis-Galand d'Olabaratz.

D'Olabaratz's precise origins are unknown. He was born early in the century, somewhere in the French Basque country, perhaps at Saint

Jean Frédéric Phélypeaux, Comte de Maurepas, French Minister of Marine.

Jean de Luz, and came to Île Royale like many of his compatriots to pursue the fishery. Granted land at Louisbourg in 1722, he settled in the town in the 1730s and soon prospered. By 1740 he was owner of his own vessel, and when the fishery stagnated in 1744 he turned his boat to a new enterprise: attacking English shipping as a privateer.

On May 24 the French force slipped between the barren granite islands and barren granite mainland that form Canso's harbour. On either side the crude dwellings of the settlement's fishers pocked the shore, scarcely protected by a small blockhouse housing a weak garrison. Canso was still unaware of the war; it had few means to resist its attackers regardless. The French opened their assault by bombarding the blockhouse. After a perfunctory resistance by the English guard-ship, the town promptly surrendered. Loading plunder and prisoners onto their modest fleet of smacks, the expedition burned the ragged settlement to the ground before retracing the coast northwards, back to Louisbourg.

The Canso attack set the tone for the offensive of the early summer of 1744. D'Olabaratz and his fellow privateers' lightly armed vessels attacked unsuspecting targets, invariably forcing capitulation after a token resistance. In the first two weeks of June they captured at least ten vessels this way, mostly Massachusetts fishers working the nearby Canso and Sable Island banks. Boston learned of the Canso attack on June 10, and by mid-month New England vessels would no longer be surprised. Most returned south, leaving the seas off Île Royale clear of enemy shipping. Louisbourg privateers hunted their prizes thereafter in New England waters.

By July a new phase of the privateering campaign began.

American colonial privateers at Newport, c.1739. Their counter-offense against the French had serious consequences, not least for Joannis-Galand d'Olabaratz.

Louisbourg's wealthy merchants and officials bankrolled larger and more heavily armed privateers that could operate in the distant, dangerous and prize-rich approaches to New England. At the same time, the New Englanders themselves prepared a counter-offensive, building privateers that could both protect their shipping and carry the war back to the coasts of Île Royale.

One of the first to take the water was d'Olabaratz's *Cantabre*, purchased and outfitted by the privateer and three partners including Governor du Quesnel. *Cantabre* mounted eight cannon and eight swivel guns, and her punch was compounded when d'Olabaratz decided to cruise with the comparably armed *César*. *Cantabre* and *César* arrived off the Massachusetts coast at the beginning of July and were soon separated in dense fog. On June 5 and 6 *César* made three quick captures in succession, sending them back to

A view of Salem in the 18th century: one of New England's primary ports.

The snow raised its English colours in reply: the privateer knew instantly that he was trapped. His prize revealed herself as the Massachusetts coast guard *Prince of Orange*, commanded by Captain Edward Tyng and crewed by 100 New Englanders eager for revenge.

The snow immediately opened her ports, ran out her guns and fired a broadside, raking *Cantabre*'s deck. D'Olabaratz's crew returned fire. Outgunned, they broke out oars and tried to outrun *Prince of Orange* in the flat calm. An excruciating 12-hour pursuit under oars ensued, stoked by rations of spirits. *Prince of Orange* fired her bow chaser, her forwardmost gun, at *Cantabre* the whole time, scoring nine direct hits that wreaked havoc on the privateer's rigging. The New Englanders overtook d'Olabaratz at two in the morning the following day, hitting the privateer with a full broadside and constant small arms fire that brought down her mast and further wrecked her rigging. His ship ruined and unmanageable, d'Olabaratz struck his colours. Launching a boat from *Cantabre*'s choked deck, he presented his sword and commission to Tyng. Gallant in defeat, he complimented especially the skill of *Prince of Orange*'s gunners. On July 6 the coast guard towed *Cantabre* into Boston in

Louisbourg with prize crews. They arrived with much-needed cargoes of flour and oil within days of Morpain's captures, *Nancy* and *Kingsbury*, taken the same month in *Succès*. The town was elated by the continued success of its privateers.

Cantabre's cruise proceeded differently. At nine in the morning on July 4 she encountered a suspicious vessel wallowing in a calm off Cape Cod, a snow (a two-masted vessel, similar to a brig) sailing without identifying colours. As D'Olabaratz closed within cannon shot of his prize, he smartly replaced his own false colours with a French ensign.

triumph, and the town erupted in celebration. The merchants of Boston awarded Tyng an elegant silver cup in recognition of his success, grateful for having a nasty threat to their business eliminated.

Cantabre's loss signalled a turn in the tide of Louisbourg's fortunes. Henceforth French privateers brought home fewer and fewer prizes, while an ever-increasing number of New England vessels attacked the port's fishers and traders. By September they would threaten Louisbourg itself. D'Olabaratz witnessed this Yankee resurgence first-hand as a prisoner in New England. Granted remarkable freedom to travel, he saw privateers mounting 10 to 16 guns outfitting at Boston, and larger 20- to 26-gun ships under construction. The situation in Rhode Island was even more menacing: the colony's 23 privateers moved him to fury at this "pernicious place."

D'Olabaratz assessed the strength of the towns he visited in New England, developing plans of attack that he later carried to the Minister of Marine in Versailles. He learned remarkable details of the strongholds on the coast and the number and calibre of guns they mounted; the amount of powder in their magazines. A single weak fortress in the harbour mouth guarded the great, rich town of Boston; a modest force of half a dozen large frigates, he reported, could ransom it for millions. Rhode Island had no defences other than its small privateers. Philadelphia was governed by Quakers, and had no defences at all. The only town on the coast that gave d'Olabaratz pause was New York where, unlike the New England towns where each was his own master, royal government kept the population in good order. The more that English colonial towns resembled

Toulon, the principal French naval base in 1775: its bustling dockyards are a measure of the nation's strength at sea in this period.

Louisbourg, the less susceptible to attack they seemed.

D'Olabaratz reported that New England was abuzz with rumours of an expedition against Louisbourg set for the spring of 1745. The merchants of Boston, eager to destroy the privateers' nest and plunder the riches of the town, were reportedly raising large sums to pay a force of 15 Royal Navy ships and 6000 colonial militiamen. The privateer dismissed the possibility of attack: people in the countryside had no interest in the merchants' scheme and would not fight. They were, he reported, "persuaded that there were more blows to receive than coins to gain" at Louisbourg.

In September d'Olabaratz and his crew returned to Louisbourg in a prisoner exchange. His account of wartime preparations in New England offered little comfort to the people of Louisbourg as they prepared for a long, anxious winter. The Canso garrison was exchanged the same month, carrying word of the *Compagnie des Indes* fleet to Boston. On November 4 the *Indes* fleet left Louisbourg for France as part of a convoy of 53 ships, taking with them the warships that had

Jean Baptiste Louis Frédéric de la Rochefoucauld de Roye, Duc d'Anville: leader of the huge, doomed expedition to retake Louisbourg.

protected Île Royale's coasts through the autumn. Battered by storms in the Atlantic, the convoy was attacked repeatedly by the English on the passage.

D'Olabaratz likewise left Louisbourg before winter closed in, carrying his intelligence on the English colonies to Versailles. While there, he learned to his shock that the force of ragtag militias and Royal Navy professionals dismissed in his report had in fact taken Louisbourg — the strongest fortress in America — in the spring of 1745.

Plan of Annapolis.

When the French court planned a counter-attack, d'Olabaratz, with his long experience of the Acadian and New England coasts, was inevitably part of it.

The plan envisioned an overwhelming and unprecedented land-sea expedition against English interests in the western North Atlantic. It aimed to retake Louisbourg, secure the approaches to Canada and reclaim the settlements of Acadia lost to France since 1713. It would then turn south, ravaging the New England coast as far as Boston. On July 22 ten ships of the line, three frigates, two corvettes, a hospital ship, 45 troopships and merchant vessels and 3500 infantry troops — nearly 11,000 men in

Image of a Canadian militiaman: such fighters were crucial in New France's ongoing battle with New England.

The French port of La Rochelle: d'Anville's ill-fated expedition of 61 ships and 11,000 men left the anchorage of this great port in July of 1746.

all — worked their way out of Aix Roads, off Rochefort, and into the Atlantic. The entire force was under the command of Jean Baptiste Louis Frédéric de la Rochefoucauld de Roye, duc d'Anville; D'Olabaratz commanded one of the armada's smaller ships. Their projected landfall was the unsettled harbour of Chebucto, in Nova Scotia (present-day Halifax). A great many of those embarked would never make it.

Disaster struck almost immediately. Fierce storms scattered the fleet off the Azores. Single ships continued to the west as best they could, some fighting contrary Atlantic winds for months only to be hit by storms again off Sable Island. Those that survived the passage straggled into Chebucto, typhus raging through their crews. Hundreds died horribly from the disease, which was soon known among the

In 1759 and 1760 large numbers of British troops massed in the American interior, ready to strike New France's coup de grace. *Too few bold men—like d'Olabaratz—stood against them.*

postponed. D'Olabaratz succeeded Pierre Morpain as Louisbourg's port captain in 1750, working for the next eight years to ensure the town's seaward defences would be ready when the fight resumed. In the winter of 1758 the Royal Navy drew a noose around the fortress, starving it in preparation for attack. D'Olabaratz took to the waters, successfully evading the blockade to provision the beleaguered town. That summer, when Louisbourg fell to the English a second and final time, d'Olabaratz was in France receiving the Cross of Saint Louis. The very survival of New France now depended on the courage and ingenuity of men like the freshly knighted Chevalier d'Olabaratz.

The fall of Louisbourg opened the way

French as "la maladie de Chibouctou." D'Anville perished and was buried on an island in the harbour, his heart returned to his family in a lead casket. After an aborted thrust against the English at Annapolis Royal, the remnants of the wrecked expedition turned homewards. It had accomplished absolutely nothing, at immense cost.

Surviving the d'Anville expedition d'Olabaratz returned to Louisbourg, restored to France at war's end — to the disgust of the New Englanders who stormed it three years earlier. Boston and Louisbourg alike realized the final battle of France and England for America had merely been

A xebeck *or* chebeque: *these small vessels formed the core of d'Olabaratz's improvised navy.*

Portrait of Jeffrey Amherst, whose methodical advance culminated in the fall of Montreal.

View of the destruction of a French vessel on the St. Lawrence River.

for an attack on the heartland of New France, on Canada itself. As in past wars, the English plan envisioned a pincer movement to crush the colony. Forces under James Wolfe proceeded up the St. Lawrence River to attack Quebec. Overland, 11,000 soldiers under Jeffrey Amherst moved methodically northward from New York, along Lake Champlain towards Montreal. If the two forces joined in the centre of the colony, France's dream of empire in America would be crushed. In 1759, d'Olabaratz recrossed the Atlantic to confront this threat.

The privateer was soon on Lake Champlain commanding a tiny force of chébecs — open boats mounting small-calibre guns — as part of the thin line of French defences protecting Montreal. Writing to his forces on the southern front, French commander Louis Joseph de Montcalm de Saint-Véran emphasized the crucial nature of the battle to come: "We must fight for our honour, for our interests and for the final time." D'Olabaratz's force comprised only three boats, five officers and 90 men. Nevertheless, it was sufficient to halt Amherst's advance while he constructed a small navy — a brigantine, a floating battery and an armed sloop — with which to confront the French. On October 12 d'Olabaratz captured a small troop carrier, taking 21 Highlanders from the 42nd Regiment of Foot prisoner. Later that day Amherst's

Amherst's army making the dangerous descent of rapids above Montreal.

navy, big vessels mounting dozens of guns, approached. Faced with overwhelming force, d'Olabaratz scuttled his chébecs and escaped overland to Montreal with his prisoners.

D'Olabaratz's experience on Lake Champlain was typical of French military fortunes in 1759: a bold but futile attempt to improvise a defence against the enemy's overwhelming superiority of men and material. At Montreal two of the captured Highlanders — former Jacobites, veterans of the army of Bonnie Prince Charlie — described the scale of Amherst's forces, advising the French to take to the woods before they arrived. In September Quebec fell to Wolfe's attackers, and Amherst halted his ponderous advance. The following year English sea power won control of the St. Lawrence, cutting the colony's lifeline to France and ensuring its conquest. France's long struggle for empire in America had finally been crushed. With the fall of New France d'Olabaratz joined the many forced into exile, returning to his native Basque country where he died, at Bayonne, in 1778.

Chapter Six

A PRIVATEER IN THE NAVY

O n the last day of May 1745, the 64-gun French
warship *Vigilant* drove through North Atlantic fog
towards the coast of Île Royale. Riding deeply in the
heavy seas, her lower gunports barely above the foaming
waterline, she was laden with men and supplies — 500 troops,
1000 barrels of gunpowder, 40 cannon and quantities of
provisions — for relief of the fortress at Louisbourg, ever
more closely besieged by attacking New England militias. Île
Royale had been ravaged, every building on the island
plundered or destroyed, the fortress and town mauled by
batteries of artillery on every side. Besieging forces were
preparing a final, devastating assault. Inside the battered
walls Louisbourg's defenders were running short of
gunpowder, food and — increasingly — hope. The town's
survival hung in the balance.

At noon *Vigilant* encountered the 40-gun *Mermaid* and
gave chase, hoping to win the cannon of a Royal Navy

*A British ship of the line in the 1750s: while vessels of the size were seldom
seen in North American waters, British sea power made itself felt
increasingly as the century progressed.*

warship for Louisbourg's hard-pressed defenders. *Mermaid* drew the French ship northwards, towards an English fleet concealed in the fog. By late afternoon the armed snow *Shirley* joined the fray. *Vigilant* at last saw the trap laid before her. She turned and ran. *Shirley*'s gunners brought their bow-chaser to bear, tearing at the larger ship's rigging. By early evening two more English vessels, *Eltham* and *Superbe*, joined the fight, attacking the enemy with broadsides and musket fire. *Vigilant*'s crew continued to fight until her shattered hull and shredded rigging became unmanageable. When, after nightfall, the ship finally surrendered, 60 crewmen had been killed or wounded. Louisbourg's best hope of enduring the siege was lost: within the month New England forces marched into the town, victorious.

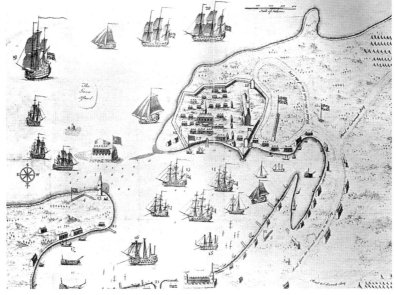

Map illustrating the disposition of American colonial ships at the siege of Louisbourg, 1745.

Mermaid, *Eltham*, and *Superbe* were Royal Navy warships of Commodore Peter Warren's fleet, strongly manned and under naval discipline. The latest provincial vessel to distinguish herself, *Shirley* was a Massachusetts provincial vessel, manned by volunteer fishers, traders and ex-privateersmen. She was one of nine vessels outfitted by the colony for the expedition to destroy Louisbourg, including the venerable *Prince of Orange* and the *Massachusetts*, whose master, Edward Tyng, had taken the Louisbourg privateer d'Olabaratz in New England waters a year earlier. *Shirley* was commanded by John Rous, one of Massachusetts' most experienced and successful privateering captains.

As a privateer, Rous had already worked closely with the Royal Navy. In June 1744 he cruised against French fishers on the Grand Banks of Newfoundland in the brig *Young Eagle*, bringing five prizes into St. John's by the end of the month. In early July he captured another nine vessels, including three large merchant ships. Royal Navy officers at Newfoundland soon recognized Rous's initiative and ability, and supplemented his crew with 50 Royal Marines on his next cruise.

Sailing in company with three other privateers on August 1, Rous hunted and attacked a force of armed French vessels at Fishott Island in northern Newfoundland. The French knew of this private squadron's approach and drew up across the harbour mouth, broadside to the enemy. A fierce, hours-long battle followed, with ships on both sides holed and rigging shambled. Rous's force prevailed, but at great cost: 11 of his men were killed, and another 30 wounded. Their prize: five vessels, ninety guns, and more fish than they could ship.

When Louisbourg fell, Commodore Warren saw a chance to reward Rous's merit and strengthen Royal Navy forces in American waters. Sending Rous with news of the Louisbourg victory to the Duke of Newcastle, the most powerful minister in the British government, Warren recommended that this "brisk, gallant man" be given a commission in the Royal Navy, to serve on the New England Station. Soon Captain John Rous, RN, returned to the New England coast in His Majesty's snow *Shirley*. It was the fitting culmination of a distinguished privateering career.

The facts of Rous's early life are obscure. He was born in New England soon after the turn of the century, and no doubt pursued a seafaring career early. In 1739 the War of Jenkin's Ear (named after the mutilation of an English seaman by Spanish *garda costa*) broke out between England and Spain, resuming imperial warfare in the Americas after a long lull. Rous signed on as first lieutenant of the Boston privateer *Young Eagle*, 100 tons, 12 carriage guns and 18 swivel guns, and under Captain Philip Dumaresq. Dumaresq maintained a strict discipline on the privateer. Soon after she departed on her first cruise in November, he firmly suppressed a budding mutiny among the crew. The experience gained on this tightly run privateer served Rous well in his later career.

In the winter of 1739-40 *Young Eagle* cruised the eastern Atlantic hunting Spanish prizes. Her first capture was a ship of 200 tons, 20 guns, sailing out of Tenerife with a mixed cargo of wheat, oil, beans, rice, olives and

Above: Portrait of Sir Peter Warren, commander of naval forces at the 1745 siege.
Below: Rous's call for a privateering crew, from a contemporary newspaper.

THE Billender *Young Eagle*, about 100 *Tons* (John Rouſe *Commander*) mounted with 10 *Carriage and* 24 *Swivel Guns*, victualled for 90 *Men*, 9 *Months*, and every way equipt for her *Cruise*, is deſign'd to ſail from this Port in 10 Days from this date ; all thoſe that have engag'd to go in ſaid Veſſel are deſired to repair on Beard. Boſton, Nov. 30. 1741. John Rouſe.

lumber. Dumaresq stayed at Madeira to oversee prize proceedings, sending *Young Eagle* back out under Rous's command.

On January 15 Rous took the sloop *Amsterdam Post* sailing out of Cork, Ireland with a cargo of fish, butter, candles, hides, hats, soap, wax and two sets of suspiciously contradictory papers. Heading back into Madeira he encountered the *St. Jean Baptiste*, heavily armed with 18 carriage guns. The master of this ship mistook Rous and his prize for two privateers hunting in consort, and struck his colours without a fight. Rous returned to Boston as part of *Amsterdam Post*'s prize crew, pleased with his initial success as a privateer captain.

Young Eagle continued her cruise through the summer of 1741 without Rous, capturing rich prizes: a French ship laden with wine, hemp, tapestry, gold lace, books and jewellery and a vessel flying Papal colours.

When Captain Dumaresq died that year, *Young Eagle* returned to Boston armed with 14 carriage guns and 42 swivels, menacing evidence of the 16 prizes she had taken. In December, Rous took command of the ship, reducing her armament to a lean, lethal 10 carriage and 24 swivel guns. With a crew of

Basseterre in St. Christopher, West Indies, in the late eighteenth century.

135 men recruited in Boston and Rhode Island, *Young Eagle* again sailed against Spanish shipping, this time in West Indian waters.

Rous again found success, but this time at a very high price. His first capture was a Rhode Island merchant sloop, *South Kingstown*, carrying a typical West Indian cargo of molasses, sugar, rum and indigo from Hispaniola under false papers. His next encounter was with a rich, heavily armed Spanish vessel bound from Spain to Cartagena. This ship fought the privateer, disabling 50 of *Young Eagle's* crew. Inspired perhaps by this experience, Rous soon arranged to sail in consort with two privateers sailing out of St. Christopher, the *Boneto* and the *Mary*, learning techniques of squadron action that characterize his career from this point onwards.

On June 29, 1742 the squadron encountered a fleet of well-armed Spanish ships off the coast of Central America and chased the largest, the *De La Clara*, until she struck her

colours. On July 15 the privateers boarded the Dutch vessel *Three Brothers*, which was trading illegally with the Spanish, capturing her volatile cargo of liquor and gunpowder. Days later they rescued the officers of the English merchantman *Alexander* from a mutinous crew. Action continued into August, as *Young Eagle* and *Boneto* pursued eight Spanish vessels for hours along the Florida coast, finally trapping four of them in an isolated bay. The two largest vessels — the *Divina Pastora* and *Nuestra Senora de los Delores y las Animas* — surrendered after a brief fight, but the two smaller ships escaped in shoal water. Three days later the privateers, flying false colours, approached five vessels and a chase ensued in heavy seas. Rous and his consorts drove three of the ships aground and salvaged their cargoes. It was a rich end to *Young Eagle's* 1742 cruise.

Rous cruised the West Indies again in 1743, taking prizes in the reef-strewn waters before returning to Boston in the

An artist's impression of New England troops embarking for Louisbourg, 1745.

Portrait of William Pepperell, colonial commander of ground forces at Louisbourg.

On Sunday April 4, 1745, 2800 New England militiamen in 51 transports departed Boston and sailed north towards the Nova Scotian coast. The day was marked with solemn prayer and fasting, moving the acerbic Benjamin Franklin to indulge in a theological speculation on the expedition's prospects. Calculating the population of Boston and the intensity of its devotion, Franklin reckoned the expedition was armed with "forty-five millions of prayers; which, set against the prayers of a few priests in the Garrison, to the Virgin Mary, give a vast balance in your favour." But the ever-practical Franklin warned against undue reliance on such prayers in earthly matters like war, noting that "in attacking strong towns I should have more dependence on works, than on faith; for, like the kingdom of heaven, they are to be taken by force and violence."

John Rous escorted the force northwards in the snow

spring of 1744 with smallpox raging through his crew. Soon, news of renewed war with France came in a barrage of ill tidings: the fall of Canso and the devastation of the fisheries by Louisbourg corsairs. New England promptly deployed provincial vessels and privateers, seeking out encounters with the French off the Nova Scotia and Massachusetts coasts. *Young Eagle* fixed her aim on French interests in Newfoundland, attacking fishing vessels and settlements of the island's north shore with devastating effect. As the year progressed New England turned to destroy the source of France's depredations in the region, its chief base in the North Atlantic — the port and fortress of Louisbourg.

Engraving of Massachusetts, *colonial flagship at Louisbourg, 1745.*

New Englanders disembark at Gabarus in their advance on the French colonial fortress.

In late April Rous, Tyng and their fellow-captains chased the fast 32-gun frigate *Renommée* off the coast. A month later Rous assisted in the capture of the heavily laden *Vigilant*, and Louisbourg's fate was sealed. On May 11 the New Englanders poured ashore at Gabarus, south of the fortress, quickly overcoming brave but inadequate French opposition. They began a bold, undisciplined advance, subjecting the fortress to relentless bombardment. At the same time they ranged throughout the island, burning and plundering everything in their path. Rous sailed constantly between Louisbourg, Annapolis and Boston, carrying armaments, provisions, fresh troops and orders, while Royal Navy and Massachusetts sea forces maintained a tight noose around the port. By the end of June, New England forces occupied the battered town.

The fall of Louisbourg was only one scene in an intensifying struggle between France and England in the western North Atlantic. In 1746 the Duc d'Anville embarked on his doomed attempt to retake Île Royale. Soon after, the Canadian governor at Quebec sent forces to occupy the Saint John River Valley and the Chignecto Isthmus, areas of

Shirley, a 20-gun Massachusetts provincial ship attached to the combined colonial-Royal Navy force commanded by Commodore Peter Warren. Two weeks after departure the expedition's undisciplined amateur troops drilled sullenly among the charred ruins of Canso, on the verge of mutiny for lack of provisions. Rous in *Shirley*, along with Tyng in the *Massachusetts*, cruised the coast for likely prey. By the end of the month they had taken two heavily laden prizes, rich in provisions, molasses and rum. The troops were contented, temporarily at least.

uncertain jurisdiction, their status subject to the deliberations of an international commission. In the winter of 1747 an expedition of Canadians marched overland through ice and snow from Chignecto to Grand Pré, where a force of New England militia was lodged among the inhabitants.

The Canadians arrived after three weeks' arduous travel and attacked the New Englanders under cover of a blizzard, shooting and bludgeoning the militiamen in their beds. Seventy men were killed, with many more wounded and taken captive. One of Rous's first duties on his return from England as a captain in the Royal Navy was to reassert English authority at this Minas Basin settlement, arriving on April 12 with a 24-gun brig, two armed schooners and a force of 300 men. Before long the New Englanders would return to Grand Pré in even greater numbers, with grievous results for the Acadians there.

In 1748 Rous returned to England in *Shirley* in mid-winter. Ship and crew were nearly obliterated in the stormy North

Halifax was founded in 1749 to assert British power in Nova Scotia and to offset that of France at Louisbourg.

Atlantic by gales so fierce they stripped the ship of sails, masts and yards, and seas so high they washed foremast sailors into the sea. In England the Royal Navy gave Rous the frigate *Albany* to replace the battered *Shirley*. They also consulted him on plans to establish a new settlement on Nova Scotia's Atlantic coast as a permanent counterweight to Louisbourg, which had been returned to the French in the treaty ending the present war — much to the disgust of the New Englanders who had stormed it.

The following year Rous in *Albany* was among those dispatched to establish the new town of Halifax, arriving to find the sunken hulks and bleached bones of d'Anville's expedition still littering the shore of the broad basin at the harbour's head. With his immense knowledge of the North Atlantic, Rous served as senior naval officer on the Nova Scotian station, watching the colony's coasts and controlling the endemic smuggling among French, English and New Englanders that helped sustain the enemy at Louisbourg.

Sailing out of the restored Île Royale fortress, France had near-constant naval supremacy in the region. The Royal Navy usually sent only two or three ships to Nova Scotian waters, which often arrived too late in the season to be of use against smugglers. Drawing on the talent for squadron work he developed while a privateering captain, and his experience in Massachusetts colonial service Rous oversaw the organization of an irregular Nova Scotian sea militia. He soon supplemented an inadequate Royal Navy presence with sloops and schooners crewed and commanded by tough local seamen, familiar with Nova Scotian seas and conditions.

Tensions between French and English continued to rise in the years after Halifax was settled, threatening to break into open conflict in the disputed borderlands of Chignecto and along the Saint John River. In June 1749 Rous sailed in *Albany* to investigate French "encroachments" on the river, finding the old French fort at its mouth — a relic of past conflicts — completely deserted. Taking a schooner at anchor there, Rous

Model of the schooner Musquodoboit, *typical of the small, manoeuvrable vessels used by colonial sea militias.*

French commander, Boishébert, strike his colours. Boishébert refused. Rous insisted, this time more forcefully. The French commander reluctantly complied. When the officers met on board *Albany,* Boishébert informed Rous that he had orders to remain in the area and prevent English settlement until its status, then the subject of diplomacy in Europe, was finally determined. This equivocal meeting opened a decade of covert and often violent thrusts and counter-thrusts on the river.

English authorities reacted to French encroachments at Chignecto as well. In May 1750 Rous escorted a force of 400 soldiers under the command of Major Charles Lawrence to the Acadian settlement of Beaubassin, investigating French activities and preparing to fortify the region. On arrival, they found the once-prosperous village burned to the ground and its population forcibly relocated to lands claimed by France, west of the narrow Missaguash River. When Lawrence spoke to the Canadian commander, the Chevalier La Corne, he received a response similar to the one that Boishébert had

sent its captain upriver with a summons to the French forces. Days later a force of Canadian and native fighters marched into sight, accompanied by military drums and French flags, emblems of sovereignty in a disputed land.

The force marched boldly to within a musket-shot of *Albany,* and halted. Rous immediately demanded that the

View of Halifax with squadron leaving for Louisbourg, 1757.

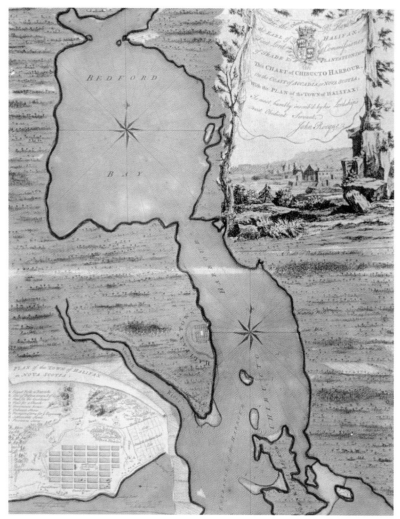

Halifax in the 1750s, showing the town's tight, military grid.

earlier offered at the mouth of the Saint John River: French forces occupied the territory to prevent English encroachment, while its final status was determined diplomatically.

In late August Rous returned to Chignecto with a flotilla of six sloops and schooners carrying troops, arms, stores, provisions, prefabricated barracks and blockhouses to plant a fort on the ruins of Beaubassin. At the same time the French began fortifying the commanding ridge of Beauséjour, little more than a mile across the marshy ground. A diplomatic solution seemed increasingly unlikely.

As open conflict with France moved inexorably nearer, Rous did what he could to maintain Nova Scotia's defences with his small force of Royal Navy and colonial vessels. In late 1750, Rous intercepted the 10-gun ship *St. Francis* and a small schooner off Nova Scotia's Cape Sable Island, carrying ammunition and provisions for French troops on the Saint John River. Firing several shots to make them heave-to, Rous instead saw the bigger vessel clear her decks for action. He promptly attacked with a broadside and musket fire. After a two-hour running battle *St. Francis* finally surrendered, her rigging destroyed, the ship completely unmanageable. Protesting the capture of one of their ships at a time of nominal peace, Louisbourg authorities seized four New England trading vessels then in port.

That year Rous also helped to establish Fort Edward at Pisquid (modern-day Windsor), close to Grand Pré and the other large Acadian settlement at Minas. In 1753 he carried "Foreign Protestant" settlers to the new town of Lunenburg, as part of an attempt to counter the demographic dominance of the French-speaking, Catholic Acadian population. In 1754 he was appointed to Nova Scotia's governing council, where he was responsible for many crucial decisions regarding the colony's future.

At Chignecto, fortification of the disputed frontier between English and French continued. By 1755 the rival strong points of Fort Lawrence and Fort Beauséjour glowered at each other across the marshlands at the head of the Bay of Fundy. In Massachusetts Governor Shirley determined it was time to dislodge the French from their encroachments, and an expedition was duly organized. Rous departed Boston on May 22 in the 20-gun ship *Success*, commanding a squadron of three warships, six store ships and 22 transports loaded with New England militiamen bound to besiege Beauséjour.

The expedition advanced like clockwork: landing at Chignecto in the first days of June, marching on the fort, building siege batteries, opening a bombardment. Watching the campaign from the deck of his ship, Rous mused light-heartedly in a letter to his friend Colonel John Winslow about his wish to be ashore: "If you have any good saddle horses in your stable I should be obliged to you for one to ride round the ship's deck for exercise, for I am not likely to

have any other." Beauséjour fell in mid-June. On July 25, 1755, Nova Scotia's governing council met to consider the fate of the Acadians, determining that they would have to take an unqualified oath of allegiance to the English Crown on pain of being removed from the colony. Rous and Winslow's levity disappeared: both were

Top: British forces landing above Cape Diamond before the attack on Quebec, 1759. Rous was a member of the naval contingent.
Bottom: After siege, bombardment, and occupation, Quebec lay in ruins.

charged with enforcing the governing council's resolution. Winslow was sent to oversee the destruction of the ancient settlements at Minas. Rous escorted a convoy of 900 Chignecto Acadians into exile in the Carolinas.

John Rous's final years matched the last days of France's empire in America. In 1758 he commanded the 50-gun ship *Sutherland*, sailing reconnaissance missions out of Halifax to assess French naval strength at Louisbourg. As English forces prepared to attack, Rous served in the Royal Navy's blockading force under Admiral Boscawen, returning to the scene of his early successes in *Shirley* 13 years earlier. When Louisbourg fell and English forces poured into the St. Lawrence, at last attacking the heartland of New France, Rous sailed with them. Arriving off the citadel of Quebec, he was chosen to lead a

squadron of ships upriver under the town's guns, flanking it and dividing its defences. On the night of September 12, 1759 British troops embarked in landing barges from *Sutherland*, commencing a bold assault that culminated in James Wolfe's epochal victory over Montcalm at the Plains of Abraham. The end of New France had begun.

This was Rous's last campaign. In December the old privateer and Royal Navy officer escorted one final convoy across the wintry North Atlantic to England. There he died, at the great naval harbour of Portsmouth, on April 3, 1760.

Left: Portrait of James Wolfe, conquerer of Quebec.

View of H. M. Dockyard, Plymouth, England. Rous spent his last year on England's south coast and died at another great naval base nearby, Portsmouth.

Chapter Seven

A SEA RANGER

In autumn 1750 the parallel ridges dominating the disputed borderlands between Nova Scotia and New France were crested with rival French and English forts — Beauséjour and Lawrence. While imperial tensions rose, a sort of practical détente grew between the two posts, separated by a mile and a half of marshland and the muddy trickle of the Missaguash River. Rival officers regularly agreed to exchange deserters and met to discuss prisoners held on either side. Then, on October 15, Captain Edward How walked out under a flag of truce to speak with French officers on the banks of the river. When the parley concluded and How turned to leave, fighters concealed on the bank stood and fired at close range, shooting him through the heart and killing him. English authorities were

outraged. It was, according to Nova Scotia's governor Edward Cornwallis, "An instance of treachery and barbarity not to be paralleled in history."

The English were quick to assign blame. How's death, they claimed, was the responsibility of Jean-Louis Le Loutre, French missionary to the Mi'kmaq and Acadians, a man who for years had actively thwarted English plans for Nova Scotia. Le Loutre arrived in the colony in 1737, studying the Mi'kmaq language and travelling tirelessly among native and Acadian settlements. When war broke out between France and England in 1744, he encouraged guerrilla attacks and helped

In the 1750s Atlantic Canada became the front line of European imperial conflict—on land and at sea.

coordinate French ground and naval forces in the region. That year he was with Joseph Dupont Du Vivier's forces besieging Annapolis Royal and he joined the mauled remnants of d'Anville's fleet at Chebucto in 1746. At the fall of Louisbourg in 1745, Commodore Peter Warren and Massachusetts militia commander William Pepperell tried to lure him into captivity with promises of protection. He wisely escaped to Quebec instead. By 1750 Le Loutre was a key figure in the region, working tirelessly and sometimes brutally to convince neutral Acadians to move to French territory, and the Mi'kmaq to remain hostile to English authority.

A 19th century portrait of Jean-Louis Le Loutre, missionary priest, warrior and fugitive. So disruptive was his influence that Nova Scotian Governor Cornwallis put a bounty on his life.

Cornwallis proclaimed a bounty of £50 for his capture and then plotted more active measures to bring the militant priest's work to an end.

One of Cornwallis's preferred agents for such measures was Captain Sylvanus Cobb, master of the sloop *York*. To deter further attacks on English interests, Cornwallis hired Cobb and his vessel to raid and burn the French settlements at Chignecto, capture Le Loutre and as many enemy fighters as possible and, if necessary, take the women and children hostage. *York* sailed with letters from Cornwallis outlining the project to Massachusetts' governor Phips at Boston, where Cobb was to victual and provision his vessel and recruit men for the expedition. These letters described Cobb approvingly as a settler in Nova Scotia, "thoroughly acquainted with every harbour and creek in the Bay [of Fundy] and who knows every house in Chignecto." In short, a man perfectly suited to the task. While Cobb advertised for volunteers in Boston, Cornwallis became concerned that the French had learned of the attack and called it off. Five years later, when English authorities would finally confront Le Loutre, Cobb would be close at hand.

Sylvanus Cobb was born in the old coastal town of Plymouth, Massachusetts in 1710. Like many able and ambitious New Englanders of his generation he joined the 1745 expedition against the French fortress of Louisbourg, serving as an officer with Massachusetts land forces. He

Portrait of Edward Cornwallis, Governor of Nova Scotia: Cornwallis's campaign against French and First Nations fighters was extreme and unscrupulous.

remained in the occupied town after its fall, charged with salvaging vessels sunk in the captured town's harbour during the siege. In the following years he was stationed in the old Nova Scotian capital of Annapolis Royal, from where he reinforced the Grand Pré garrison a month before it was attacked by French forces in 1747. Soon he shifted operations from land to sea, carrying dispatches from the governor at Annapolis and assisting with surveys of the Bay of Fundy, gaining the detailed knowledge of the Bay later praised by

Cornwallis. Soon Cobb and his vessel *York* were sailing with Captain John Rous's sea militia, clashing repeatedly with the French enemy in the ensuing decade.

A year after Rous's inconclusive 1749 cruise to the Saint John River, Cobb sailed in company with HMS *Hound* to intercept supplies bound for enemy forces. Arriving off the river's mouth he discovered and boarded a brigantine at anchor, loaded with provisions and men. Cobb and his crew embarked in a whaleboat for a reconnaissance of the inner harbour, rowing inland until they reached the site of the old French fortifications, remnants of Queen Anne's War at the turn of the century. There they found French colours flying over the dilapidated structure, now occupied by a force of some 250 fighters. Cobb unwisely landed for a parley and was promptly taken prisoner. Soon released, he was forced to reflect that French views of sovereignty on the river had hardened since Rous's visit. Returning French hostility in kind, Cobb carried six of the brigantine's crew captive to Halifax.

After the founding of Halifax in 1749, both French and English hardened their positions on the disputed frontiers of Chignecto and along the Saint John River, building new strongpoints and strengthening others. For a decade Cobb and *York* acted as a lifeline to the scattered settlements of Nova Scotia — Halifax, Annapolis and Pisquid (modern-day Windsor) — adding to his extensive and intimate knowledge of the colony's coasts. In 1752 he transported Colonel Robert Monckton to the post of Fort Lawrence. The following year he transported settlers to the new town of Lunenburg, shielding them from attack; he regularly provisioned British forces on the Chignecto isthmus, eventually building a house there for his wife and daughter.

By 1754 long-simmering tensions in the region began to boil over. The French worked ever more diligently to strengthen their positions at Beauséjour and along the Saint John River. The English worked diligently to prevent it. In

A British naval brigantine, the type of small vessel was commonly employed in American waters.

April 1755 Cobb intercepted the schooner *Marguerite* at Port La Tour off Nova Scotia's South Shore, bound from Louisbourg to Saint John with military stores and provisions. Blockading her until Royal Navy assistance arrived, he participated in her capture and received a share of the prize when the schooner was condemned and sold.

The main action of 1755 was at Beauséjour itself. By 1755, the French fort was a compact pentagon of defensive earthworks, mounting 26 cannon and protected from enemy fire by bombproof casements. In the damp, late spring, 2000 New England militiamen commanded by Plymouth native Colonel John Winslow arrived in the basin off the fort, protected by John Rous's squadron. On landing, the New Englanders joined Robert Monckton's 500 British regulars and prepared to advance on the fort. Winslow assumed quarters at Cobb's home, finding the hospitality there a welcome contrast to the chill of the surrounding marshlands. One officer reported Cobb's house well stocked with cattle, sheep, pigs ("enough to furnish the spit...every day for six months") and 400 gallons of good French wine. Very few on either side of Beauséjour's walls would enjoy such luxuries in the coming days.

Monckton and Winslow's forces began their advance across the marshes separating French and English positions on June 4, building roads to carry their heavy artillery across

The high ridge of Beauséjour, surmounted by its strong, octagonal fort, rises from the Chignecto marshlands.

Portrait of Colonel John Winslow, leader of New England forces against Beauséjour and one of the chief agents of the Acadian Expulsion.

Portrait of Robert Monckton, commander of British forces at the siege of Fort Beauséjour.

The earthworks and lichen-covered curtain wall as they appear today, Fort Beauséjour.

the sodden ground. Reaching the *de facto* border — the narrow Missaguash River — they met fierce resistance from a French party sheltering in a redoubt at the crossing. The ensuing exchange of musketry killed and wounded men on both sides. The English brought up field cannon and fired on the blockhouse, causing the French to set it ablaze and retreat, keeping up a steady fire all the while. By the end of the day the attackers occupied a ridge overlooking Beauséjour where they promptly considered the placement of siege artillery — large calibre cannon, 8- and 13-inch mortars — that would soon tear the fort apart.

Cobb now moved to supply the besieging forces' camp, running inland with vital stores and provisions under the very guns of the fort. On June 6 he sailed up the turbid Missaguash, swollen by the Bay of Fundy's immense tides. French defenders opened fire with cannon and lined the dykes at the river's edge, peppering his vessel with musket fire. Cobb's men returned fire and skirmishing parties poured out of the English camp, driving the French back behind the fort's walls. In the following days Cobb repeatedly made this dangerous passage. By June 10 all artillery and stores were upriver and in place. Beauséjour's days were numbered.

Picket at site of Fort Lawrence, looking across the marshlands toward Beauséjour.

On June 13 a force of 500 men hauled artillery forward, staking an advance position from which to open the bombardment. Eager for action, Cobb joined the party as a volunteer. Leaving at dusk, the force drove teams of oxen hauling the heavy mortars over difficult ground. They dug positions for the guns under cover of darkness, 50 men working flat on their bellies while marksmen covered them from enemy fire. Dawn rose with steady rain. Soon after, artillery reports echoed down the drenched ridge to the marshes below and out into the basin. From the deck of his ship, Rous watched the cannon and mortar shells descend on the fort, noting that the colossal 13-inch mortars hadn't yet been fired.

Beauséjour's defenders replied in kind, pouring cannon fire on the attacking battery with startling speed and precision. On the fourteenth their guns knocked an 8-inch mortar out of action. Two days later, however, the 13-inch mortars started to fire, blasting great holes in the fort's defences. One of its bombproof shelters was shattered, killing four French officers and an Englishman held prisoner in the fort. With no hope of relief and the spectre of more death and destruction before them, Beauséjour's garrison capitulated on June 16. Granted the honours of war by the victorious attackers, they marched out with their drummers drumming, shouldering small arms and with colours flying. Transported to Louisbourg, they vowed not to bear arms against the English for six months.

The Acadians of Chignecto, having lived between contending empires for a hundred years, would not receive such honourable treatment. In early August Winslow learned that the French-speaking inhabitants of Nova Scotia had refused to take an unconditional oath of allegiance to the King of England, and so would be removed from their homes and dispersed among the English-speaking colonies of America. He summoned the male inhabitants of the Chignecto settlements to surrender their arms, and

Twentieth century painting of Acadians gathered at Grand Pré church, prior to the Expulsion.

dispatched parties to destroy Acadian villages at Tatamagouche and Cobequid. The systematic expulsion of the Acadian people had begun.

The men of Chignecto who responded to Winslow's summons were kept under the guns of the captured fort, while the terrible news that their property was forfeit to the king was read to them. Many who realized the implications of the summons escaped to the forests surrounding the Chignecto marshes. English parties scoured the landscape for those who ran.

In late August a force of 200 men boarded Sylvanus Cobb's *York* and another provincial vessel, *Warren*, in an expedition to destroy Acadian settlements to the west of Chignecto. They landed first at the settlements bordering Shepody Bay, taking women and children prisoner. The men had disappeared into the woods. The soldiers systematically destroyed the settlement, ruining crops and fodder, burning houses, barns, granaries and even the church — 181 buildings in all.

They marched up the Petitcodiac River, burning every structure for 15 miles along the north bank before crossing the stream and ranging 6 miles along the south. As they approached a church, preparing to burn it, they found

Nineteenth century engraving of the embarkation of Acadians, as they are driven into exile in distant ports.

themselves encircled by a superior force of Acadians and native fighters. The English had no choice but to run, retreating under constant, deadly fire. Soon they were pinned down by fighters firing from behind dykes along the riverside, and waited for the rising tide so their transports could pass up the shallow river. Two officers and six soldiers were dead, another ten wounded. At high tide *York* and *Warren* arrived with swivel guns firing, taking the retreating forces off in boats under a continuing hail of musketry.

The expulsion of the Acadians continued in all its terror through the autumn and early winter of 1755, with whole families and communities uprooted from their homes and transported to alien lands. After his service at Beauséjour, John Winslow was ordered to destroy the large Acadian communities of the Minas Basin. He was torn by this awful duty, scarred by the sight of families who "went off

BEAUBASSIN

LE VILLAGE ACADIEN DE
BEAUBASSIN FUT FONDÉ À
CET ENDROIT PAR DES
COLONS DE PORT—ROYAL
VERS 1672. À L'ARRIVÉE
DU MAJOR CHARLES
LAWRENCE ET SES
TROUPES ANGLAISES EN
AVRIL 1750, LES
AUTORITÉS FRANÇAISES
DECIDÈRENT DE
DÉTRUIRE LE VILLAGE
AFIN DE FORCER LES
ACADIENS DE DÉMÉNAGER
AU CÔTÉ FRANÇAIS DE LA
RIVIÈRE MÉSAGOUÈCHE.
AINSI, BEAUBASSIN FUT
INCENDIÉ PAR LES
AMÉRINDIENS SOUS LA
DIRECTION PROBABLE DU
PÈRE GERMAIN ET L'ABBÉ
LE LOUTRE.

THE ACADIAN VILLAGE OF
BEAUBASSIN ON THIS SITE
WAS FOUNDED BY
SETTLERS FROM PORT ROYAL
AROUND 1672.
UPON THE ARRIVAL OF
MAJOR CHARLES
LAWRENCE WITH BRITISH
TROOPS IN APRIL 1750, THE
FRENCH AUTHORITIES HAD
THE VILLAGE DESTROYED
IN ORDER TO FORCE THE
ACADIANS TO MOVE TO THE
FRENCH SIDE OF THE
MISSAGUASH RIVER.
THUS, BEAUBASSIN WAS
BURNED BY INDIANS
LIKELY UNDER THE
DIRECTION OF FATHER
GERMAIN AND L'ABBÉ
LE LOUTRE

Monument marking the site of the Acadian settlement at Beaubassin, destroyed by French-English rivalry in the Chignecto borderlands.

solentarily and unwillingly, the women in great distress carrying off their children in their arms...others carrying their decrepit parents in their carts and all their goods moving in great confusion and appeared a screen of woe and distress." Perhaps mindful of his experience on the Petitcodiac, Cobb wrote to Winslow with harder sentiments: "I hope you will continue in such success 'til you have routed all such enemies from the land, we have not been so lucky here as so many got off before we could lay hands on them but hope to have them in time..."

Admiral Boscawen, commander of British naval forces at the second siege of Louisbourg, in 1758.

The loss of Beauséjour and the expulsion of the Acadians were traumatic, but were merely opening scenes in the last act of France and England's long imperial drama in America. In 1758, events shifted to a familiar theatre — Louisbourg. Hoping to clear the way for an attack on Quebec and the Canadian heartland, Britain prepared to attack the fortress a second time. As an overwhelming land and sea force marshalled offshore, Robert Monckton — remembering his service at Chignecto — selected Cobb to carry the brilliant, impetuous commander James Wolfe close inshore for a reconnaissance of French positions. Legend maintains that Cobb took Wolfe in very close indeed, under hot fire, causing the officer to exclaim

Thomas Davies' visual record of the "Plundering and burning of the city of Grymross, Capital of the Neutral Settlements, on the River St. John's in the Bay of Fundy, Nova Scotia." These mopping-up operations against Acadians, Canadians and the First Nations allies were especially brutal.

onshore. This time, overawed by the scale of the force appearing before them, the French retreated, warning settlements upriver of the blow that approached.

Monckton prepared to ascend the river, dispatching Cobb to Chignecto for additional small craft and pilots with local knowledge. In the third week of October the expedition got underway with nearly 1200 men, provisioned for a weeks-long hunt for the vestiges of French power in the valley. Cobb carried the commander Monckton on board, barely evading disaster in the treacherous

"Well, Cobb! I shall never doubt but you will carry me near enough!"

Cobb met Monckton again in the autumn of 1758, joining an expedition against Canadians and Acadian refugees in the Saint John River valley. Determined to shatter New France's southern flank, the English came in overwhelming force with 2000 troops, including bush-hardened Rangers and an artillery detachment. On September 11, five transports departed Halifax, escorted by Cobb in *York*, the provincial sloop *Ulysses* and the Royal Navy's *Squirrel*. On the eighteenth they reached the mouth of the river. Cobb was sent to investigate the inner harbour. As with his visit to the same spot in 1750, a force of some 200 French and natives watched

The great West Indian port of Havana, with merchant ships. The town was repeatedly besieged by rival imperial powers.

Reversing Falls at the river's mouth.

The expedition reached the Acadian refugee village of Grimross (near modern-day Gagetown) on November 4, landing a force of 700 men. No-one was there. Monckton ordered the village destroyed, houses and crops burned and livestock slaughtered. The soldiers marched upriver, through the forest, killing and burning as they went. Rangers scoured the forest for livestock to slaughter, destroying anything that could support human life. Ascending the river like a scourge, they were finally stopped by shoal water below the village of St. Anne's (modern-day Fredericton), near the site of the old Acadian capital, Nashwaak. Turning, they descended the river, destroying what had

Cobb died laying siege to Havana in 1762. The Cuban city of Havana was one of the richest prizes in the European struggle for colonial empire.

escaped their first, terrible pass. On November 8, ten days after the expedition's departure, Cobb sailed out the river mouth into the Bay of Fundy, leaving a landscape of burned houses, charred fields and rotting stock in his wake. In a week, the lush Saint John River valley had been made uninhabitable. Little by little France was being brutally dispossessed of her stake in America.

Cobb was engaged in imperial service elsewhere when British forces moved into the Saint Lawrence in 1759 and finally took the ancient citadel of Quebec. For a time he again surveyed the Nova Scotian coast, this time investigating sites for New England settlers to take the Acadians' place as the colony's productive population. In 1760 he built a home in Liverpool, a new settlement on the Atlantic coast south of Halifax that was destined to embody his hard seafaring spirit in generations of famous privateers. Two years later Cobb was dead, felled by sickness along with hundreds of his comrades while besieging Havana. He died as he lived — on campaign.

Chapter Eight

NOVA SCOTIA BESIEGED

On a raw spring morning in April 1778, the 32-gun
Royal Navy frigate HMS *Blonde* cruised the granite
coast of Nova Scotia's South Shore, combing its coves
and bays for rebel privateers. In the three years after war
erupted between Britain and its American colonies, dozens of
private armed vessels — large and small, licit and illicit —
swarmed Nova Scotia's coasts, boarding and burning fishing
vessels, preying on shipping in and out of Halifax and
plundering isolated towns. *Blonde*'s crew were nevertheless
surprised on this morning to see a large, deeply laden vessel
sailing a southward course with no flags to identify her. They
were even more surprised when, as *Blonde* approached, she
raised a French ensign, broke off her course and ran in
towards the coast under full sail.

Nova Scotia's South Shore was then notorious as a haven
for rebels. Open to the Atlantic and handy to enemy
privateering ports, it was populated largely by ex-New
Englanders whose loyalty was suspected by authorities in
Halifax. In the three decades since British soldiers and New
England militias had burned Acadian settlements and sent
their inhabitants into exile, Nova Scotia had welcomed

*A 38-gun frigate, c.1770. This type of naval vessel—exemplified by HMS
Blonde—was the powerful workhorse of North American waters.*

Benjamin Franklin in France. His electrifying presence did much to influence France's eventual intervention in the American Revolutionary War.

allegiance of the people of Liverpool, Barrington and Yarmouth couldn't be taken for granted, especially when rebel privateers cruised unmolested or even abetted, off these towns.

Blonde tracked her mystery ship, the French frigate *Duc de Choiseul*, 24 guns, to the northeast, from Port Roseway towards Liverpool Bay. After a four-hour chase the French ship struck the rocky bottom off Herring Cove, near present-day Brooklyn, and stuck fast. Her crew prepared to fight on the ship's shambled decks, but when the vessels finally engaged it became clear the British frigate would maul the marooned Frenchmen. The *Duc de Choiseul's* commander struck her colours.

Boarding their prize, British officers found her crew "drunken and insolent." They also found a complete armoury bound for rebel forces fighting in Virginia and Pennsylvania: cannon, muskets, powder and shot, clothing and equipment for 5000 men-at-arms. This was a very disturbing find. In April 1778 France hadn't openly declared its support for the American Revolutionary cause. *Duc de Choiseul* had left the French port of Nantes in mid-March as part of a plan masterminded by

thousands of migrants from Massachusetts, Connecticut and Rhode Island. These settlers now accounted for three-quarters of the province's population. They wrote letters and paid visits to family in their former colonies. Their preachers travelled back and forth to New England. They traded as often with Boston as with Halifax. For authorities in Nova Scotia — the last loyal British colony in North America — the

Pierre Augustin Caron de Beaumarchais — the famous playwright, adventurer and libertine — to supply the American rebellion covertly. The ship's course after she encountered *Blonde* — towards the Nova Scotian coast, rather than the open sea — led some to wonder whether Nova Scotians, with their suspect loyalties, were complicit in Beaumarchais's scheme.

By this time in the American Revolutionary War, Liverpool's townspeople were hard-pressed on all sides. Whatever the concerns about loyalty, Halifax authorities had done little to protect the outport from attack by rebel privateers. In October 1776 an armed schooner out of Marblehead, Massachusetts entered the port, boldly carrying off a schooner owned by the colonel of the local militia, Simeon Perkins; in March of the following year privateers carried off the cannon mounted to guard the harbour mouth; in September another schooner was seized from Perkins' wharf. The burden of these depredations was worsened when the town was forced to billet 100 sullen French sailors from the *Duc de Choiseul.*

On the first Sunday of their captivity, French Catholic officers and men in their tattered finery trooped to worship in Liverpool's austere Congregationalist meeting house. It was a bizarre sight for the townspeople, but the novelty soon wore off, as they struggled to feed a host of strangers at the end of a long, hungry winter. Perkins found them hard bread and salt meat, supplementing this standard naval fare with turnips that had survived the winter uneaten.

While *Duc de Choiseul*'s crew enjoyed Liverpool hospitality,

Simeon Perkins, Liverpool, Nova Scotia, merchant and chronicler of the town's privateering age.

Blonde's men struggled to retrieve the cache of French arms from the bottom of the frigid bay. Failing in their attempts to free and refloat the wreck the British cut holes in its side, hauling stores out of the flooded hold for more than two weeks. When *Blonde* departed on May 12 the job was far from complete, and Perkins was charged to continue the salvage. As soon as the frigate left the bay and shaped a course eastward for Halifax, however, two rebel privateers — *Washington* and *Lizard* — descended on the wreck, reclaiming the salvage for the revolutionary cause.

Liverpool, isolated and with her artillery plundered, could do little. Perkins visited *Washington*'s officers and was well received. Soon, however, the privateers turned surly and pillaged houses in the town. When the Americans at last left the bay Perkins continued the salvage, but the rebels returned, stealing stores arduously dragged from the harbour bottom. Liverpool had had enough: when *Washington* again returned she was met with musket and swivel-gun fire, and the privateers were driven off. Regardless, when *Blonde* returned, her British officers were dismayed that Perkins had passed military stores to

Reproduction flintlock pistol from Queens County Museum, Liverpool, Nova Scotia.

Above: George Washington's entry into New York marked the end of British hopes for victory in the war; in the preceding years, Nova Scotia's outposts felt the sting of rebel attacks.
Inset: New York.

after the outbreak of open war at Lexington and Concord, Halifax was struck by mysterious arsons: haystacks supplying British forces were burned and fires blazed close to the navy's dockyard. The town was dangerously vulnerable, garrisoned by a mere 36 soldiers. Its artillery was unusable, and its crude fortifications were rotting away. Loyal Halifax quaked for its safety from the first day of the Revolution.

Subsequent events transformed worry into outright panic. To the southwest, the Maine border village of Machias simmered and boiled over. Like many Nova Scotian settlements Machias was settled by New Englanders in the 1760s, and the town's economy was wrecked by an unstable political climate before 1775. Its people — like the Presbyterian minister James Lyon, formerly of Cobequid, Nova Scotia — became militant partisans of the American rebellion. In June 1775 they attacked and captured two sloops, *Unity* and *Polly*, and boldly used them to chase and capture the Royal Navy schooner *Margaretta*. It was the first rebel naval victory of the Revolution. Machias patriots soon outfitted the three vessels as privateers, setting them loose on loyal shipping in the Bay of Fundy.

In the eyes of official Halifax, the Machias attack was the most audacious outbreak in a wave of rebellion radiating outward from Philadelphia and Boston to the settlements of the Maine borderlands, the villages of the Saint John River, the prosperous farmlands of the old Acadian heartlands, and the fishing towns of Nova Scotia's South Shore. In August the Machias privateer Stephen Smith burned Fort Frederick at the mouth of the Saint John River, capturing the garrison and a brig, *Loyal Briton*. Passamaquoddy and Maugerville, in what was then far western Nova Scotia (which at the time included present-day New Brunswick), declared openly for the revolution. Known rebel sympathizers from the turbulent

the rebels, even under clear duress. In their eyes Liverpool's people were still New Englanders, after all, and capable of collusion.

Liverpool was not the only town to suffer greatly in the first years of the American Revolution. American privateers plundered settlements throughout Nova Scotia. Authorities in distant Halifax often concluded that their inhabitants were complicit in these attacks. Indeed, at times the homes of prominent loyalists seemed conspicuously more prone to attack than those of rebel sympathizers. Early in the struggle Halifax itself was subject to rebellious outbursts — it too was populated largely by New Englanders. As tensions between Britain and her colonies rose before 1775, Haligonians expressed their hostility towards increasingly distant and autocratic British rule. In the spring and summer of 1775,

Charlottetown harbour was a distinctly peaceful place, until November 17, 1776, when American privateers ransacked the town.

Below: Charlottetown in a more peaceful moment: Looking Out to Sea from Point Pleasant.

Chignecto settlements held seats in the Province's legislative assembly. Halifax's great fear — an American invasion up the Bay of Fundy to Windsor and overland to the capital — was prepared at Machias but later deferred in favour of a rebel invasion of Quebec.

Privateering attacks grew more bold and frequent. In October and November 1776 the armed schooners *Hancock* and *Franklin* out of Beverly, Massachusetts preyed on Canso's fisheries and by mid-month were in the Gulf of St. Lawrence, harassing settlements on St. John's Island (present-day Prince Edward Island). On November 17 they entered the harbour of Charlottetown and landed an armed party, threatening to burn the town unless provided with sufficient loot. They plundered houses, including that of Attorney General Phillips Callbeck, taking carpets, mirrors, bedding, furniture, liquor — and finally the attorney general himself — all before the eyes of his pregnant wife. Callbeck later complained bitterly to George Washington himself. The general apologized and relieved the offending captains of their privateering commands.

The privateers' land attacks on out-settlements stoked the rising panic in Halifax. In September colonial authorities demanded the entire population take an oath of allegiance. In December they declared martial law, on the same day that

Halifax during the Revolutionary War: the port was at times glutted with ships and troops, and others vulnerable and nearly deserted.

Montreal fell to the rebels. In April of the following year they cancelled a supreme court session in the countryside, fearing that judges in transit would be taken by privateers. At the same time British forces evacuated Boston ahead of a besieging patriot army, retreating temporarily to Halifax.

The city was suddenly jammed with regular soldiers, its defensive worries, for a time, relieved. Before returning south with his army in June 1776, British commander William Howe worked to place Nova Scotia's defences on a sounder basis. He strengthened the capital's garrison, instituted anti-privateer patrols in the Bay of Fundy and along the South Shore and manned forts at Windsor and at Cumberland (on the Chignecto Isthmus) covering the route of a potential invasion force.

Fort Cumberland (the former Fort Beauséjour, captured from the French in 1755) was especially vital. Through the winter of 1775-76 the Chignecto region seethed with rebellious sentiment. The rule of law collapsed, and loyalists lived in fear of their patriot neighbours. In June 1776 a force of fewer than 200 soldiers, mostly "fencibles," or irregular troops, arrived to occupy the crumbling ruin of the fort, immediately working to strengthen its feeble defences.

Monitoring their progress was one Jonathan Eddy, a former soldier at Beauséjour and a leader of rebel agitation in the area. In July, Eddy travelled south to the rebel capitals of Boston and Philadelphia seeking support for an invasion of Nova Scotia. He found little. In radical Machias he recruited a couple of dozen men, picking up more in Maugerville before returning north in October. As this small band approached Chignecto in early November it was joined by a force of local Acadians, still resentful of their treatment by the British 20 years earlier.

When Eddy arrived at Fort Cumberland his force comprised some 100 men, fielding small arms but no artillery. They soon captured a schooner loaded with trade goods, and then took the armed vessel *Polly* under the very guns of the fort. This was a bold move and a costly blow to British forces. In addition to the soldiers taken on board, rebels captured large quantities of provisions bound for the fort's garrison. The promise of further plunder attracted others to the rebel cause.

By the time news of the rebel attack reached Halifax, wild rumours had swelled the size of the force to 500 soldiers or more. Loyal troops marched overland to Windsor, and Royal Navy ships diverted to Cumberland Basin, countering the threatened "invasion." One of these, the sloop *Hope* under the privateer-chasing Captain James Dawson, saw fit to engage in prize-hunting en route, capturing the merchant vessel *Betsy* and returning with her to Halifax, even as Eddy and his men prepared their assault on Fort Cumberland.

The attack, when it came, was a disaster. Without American reinforcement Eddy's men were no match for an entrenched force, however feeble their entrenchment. On November 13 an attempted assault was brutally smashed by the fort's artillery, the rebels retreating in disarray. On the twenty-first they tried to burn out the garrison. Again the defenders foiled the attack. In the last days of November, as false rumours of Fort Cumberland's fall circulated in London, the garrison marched out against the besieging rebels, destroying their camp and burning the homes of prominent rebels — including Eddy's — as they went. The "invasion" of Nova Scotia was crushed. As General Washington suggested in declining to support the attack, success was impossible without naval support. This the rebel colonies simply could not provide.

Portrait of William Howe, from 1775 commander of British forces fighting the American rebels. Ultimately, he proved unequal to Washington's challenge.

If the American colonies' fledgling navy was feeble, their privateers nevertheless continued to menace Nova Scotia's isolated coastal villages. New England newspapers regularly announced vessels taken off the Nova Scotian coast. Privateers attacked fishers on the offshore banks and merchantmen in the Atlantic and Gulf of St. Lawrence. They hid among the crags of the South Shore and in the fogs of Fundy. In the summer of 1778, Kings County townships on the sheltered Minas Basin suffered repeated raids. The capital itself was not immune from attack: hostile vessels lurked in bays and coves north and south of Halifax, even venturing into the harbour's North West Arm. The lure of ships departing the town heavily laden with supplies for British armies was too tempting to resist.

Rebel privateering operations varied greatly in size,

motivation, and legality. Some privateersmen went to sea in tiny, lightly armed vessels for the sole purpose of plunder, with no regard for the niceties of law or the rules of war. At times their conduct amounted to mere vandalism. At St. John's Island, for example, vessels sailed close inshore, mauling livestock with grapeshot and leaving the corpses to rot. Other ships were large and well armed with disciplined crews, carrying commissions and treating prisoners with honour.

In November 1776 the privateer *Alfred* — under the command of John Paul Jones, the nascent American Continental Navy's first and most audacious hero — left Rhode Island for Cape Breton with the sloop *Providence* to liberate American prisoners held there. His Nova Scotia cruise proved spectacularly successful: on November 12 the American vessels took a brig bound from Liverpool to Halifax; the next day they took the transport *Mellish* off Louisbourg, bound for Canada with provisions for British

Burnham Tavern, Machias, Maine. Machias was a hotbed of Revolutionary privateering, which provided men for Eddy's failed attack on Fort Cumberland.

Engraving of John Paul Jones, the fledgling American navy's great hero who undertook devastating privateering attacks off the Cape Breton coast in late 1776.

A 1779 commemorative medal show Jones and his famous ship Bonhomme Richard *in action.*

troops there; on the sixteenth they captured a snow laden with fish; on the twenty-second *Alfred* burned a transport and the following day captured three more at Spanish River (modern-day Sydney). On the twenty-sixth they crowned the cruise with one last capture, another merchant ship bound from Liverpool to Halifax. As adept at handling prizes as winning them, Jones and his compatriots managed to sail almost all of the captured vessels safely home to New England.

The nature of privateering gave the rebels many advantages over the big, powerful ships of the Royal Navy. Throughout the war Royal Navy frigates were busy escorting convoys to and from the main theatres of war to the south, leaving the Nova Scotian coastline poorly defended. Even when on the Nova Scotia station, these ships were ill suited to chase small, shallow-draught privateers through rocky, shoal waters and narrow, craggy passages. Nevertheless, the navy did conduct successful anti-privateer patrols during the war.

Equally important to the colony's defence, especially in the out-settlements, were purely local measures: placing soldiers in strategic outposts like Lunenburg, Chester and Pictou; arming local militias, like that of Liverpool; speeding communication with the settlements with better roads; outfitting provincial vessels as a sea militia, as in earlier wars; and, of course, granting letters of marque to Nova Scotian privateers.

In the course of the war Halifax authorities issued dozens of commissions to local privateers, who outfitted vessels with evocative names like *Revenge, Dreadnought, Success, Enterprise, Halifax Bob* and *Sir George Collier*. These ships confronted their rebel counterparts, who outnumbered them, with varying success. The career of Jones Fawson, post-war High Sheriff of Halifax County, was perhaps an exception to the variable fortunes experienced by Nova Scotian privateers in the war. In 1777 he commanded the schooner *Revenge*, with 10 carriage guns, 8 swivels, and a crew of 50. The following year, cruising in the sloop *Howe* and with Captain William Callaghan in *Gage*, he took several prizes and retook a brig, *Davis*, from a prize crew off the rebel warship *Hornet*. *Hornet* had previously captured *Davis* as the brig sailed from London to Halifax. In November *Howe* and *Gage* fell in with the Salem privateer *Lively* off Jeddore, along Nova Scotia's Eastern Shore. After a two-hour chase *Howe*'s men finally boarded and captured *Lively*, her 13 swivel guns, and her crew of 16. Among those taken prisoner was the rebel privateer's captain, David Ropes. He did not remain captive long.

In 1779 the Royal Navy finally drew the rebel privateers into a full-scale battle, striking a shattering blow. In June British forces landed along Maine's Penobscot River near the Baron de Saint-Castin's old home at modern-day Castine, to establish an anti-privateer base from which to conduct operations against the Massachusetts coast. The rebellious colonies immediately mounted an expedition to dislodge the British. It was a huge, coordinated effort:

government ships from Massachusetts, New Hampshire and the fledgling Continental Navy, a dozen privateers, 22 transports and 2500 troops, including an artillery detachment commanded by the famous patriot Paul Revere.

Arriving at the Penobscot River on July 25, the force met stubborn resistance from the entrenched British and soon bogged down. The privateers grew increasingly anxious in the narrow river, with little room to manoeuvre or run. On August 3 a Royal Navy squadron dispatched by Sir George Collier sailed northwards from New York, comprising seven well-armed and manned warships, including the North American veteran HMS *Blonde*. The squadron arrived off the Penobscot on the thirteenth and sighted the enemy the next day. The Americans hurriedly re-embarked their besieging

Jones and Bonhomme Richard *engaging the enemy.*

A modern painting of American privateers landing prior to their attack on Lunenburg, Nova Scotia.

troops and prepared to fight, or to flee.

The rebel squadron mounted more than 300 cannon, the British fewer than 200. The well-trained, well-disciplined Royal Navy force promptly engaged the motley collection of privateers and militia. After an initial exchange of fire, the American fleet panicked and fell apart, its ships fleeing desperately upriver. The British gave chase, boarding and taking two of the rebels. The Americans set their vessels ablaze to keep them from enemy hands, their crews escaping overland under fire from the British ships' guns. The Americans lost 41 vessels, including 19 armed for war, and nearly 500 men. The rout on the Penobscot proved the Americans' worst naval defeat of the entire Revolutionary War.

The destruction of so many American privateers freed

Nova Scotia from the scourge of rebel attack for nearly a year. The colony's coastwise shipping resumed, and its fishers worked the offshore banks unmolested. By the spring of 1780, however, privateering raids resumed with a fierceness sharpened by a desire for revenge. In September 1780 Salem privateers again descended on Liverpool, seizing its fort and taking townspeople hostage. In August 1781 two privateer schooners attacked Annapolis Royal with a force of 80 men, capturing the town's blockhouse and pillaging everything of value — furniture, plate, linens, clothing, food, the silver buckles from ladies' shoes — before spiking the fort's guns and departing with prominent citizens as hostages. The same month, fiery revivalist preacher Henry Alline was taken on board a rebel ship. His reflections on the event undoubtedly echo that of many fellow Nova Scotians: "Let them that wish well to their souls flee from privateers as they would from the jaws of hell, for methinks a privateer may be called a floating hell." But how could people flee when American privateers

View of the Old Blockhouse, Lunenburg, c.1800.

View of Lunenburg from the southwest, painted in the decades after the American attack.

brought the war to their villages, to their very homes?

The following summer the people of Lunenburg had nowhere to flee as the late-war frenzy for plunder brought a "floating hell" to their harbour. Early on a Monday morning, July 1, 1782, Magdalena Schwartz walked out to her barn on the outskirts of Lunenburg to milk her cow. Looking to the east she saw armed men landing along the shore and

immediately roused the town to an impending attack. Colonel Creighton of the town's militia and several soldiers manned the blockhouse and fired on the attackers, wounding several. In response the Americans separated into several parties, spiking the town's cannon and destroying

Silver coffee pot that survived the town's sacking: this fine piece is indicative of the wealth of some of the townspeople.

outlying defences. Overcoming the initial resistance, they captured the colonel and his men and confined them to ships anchored off the town. They then destroyed Creighton's belongings and burned his house to the ground.

So began a systemic, day-long assault on the town. Four American privateering vessels — *Scammell, Hero, Dolphin,* and *Swallow* — and 90 men ("brave sons of liberty," according to a contemporary American account) had descended on Lunenburg. Having silenced the defenders, they brought cannon ashore and mounted them on high ground, commanding the town's tight grid of streets and the roads leading from the countryside. They then searched every house in the town, destroying weapons and taking whatever property — clothes, furniture and silver — attracted them. Resisters' homes were burned. The town's stores and warehouses were likewise plundered, yielding quantities of dry goods, beef, pork, flour and, most precious, twenty puncheons of West Indian rum.

The attackers demanded a large ransom to preserve the town from complete destruction, which was promptly paid. By late in the day, when the privateers finally reboarded their vessels and sailed out of Lunenburg Harbour, the town had been thoroughly sacked. According to one contemporary account, the townspeople "saw the privateers under sail, going out, deeply loaded with plunder...having before their departure nailed up the guns, taken away all the powder and burned the old block-house upon the hill. Indeed...they swept the town pretty well; all the shops, which were full of spring goods, are now empty; and few houses escaped being plundered...."

In the late spring of 1782 the Royal Navy also suffered a serious setback off the Nova Scotia coast. In mid-May HMS *Blonde, Duc de Choiseul*'s executioner, struck and sank on Seal Island, a notorious ships' graveyard 18 miles off the colony's southernmost coast. All but one of her crew got off alive, but they were marooned with little prospect of rescue. Within days two American privateers, *Lively* of Salem and *Scammell* of Boston (a veteran of the Lunenburg attack), appeared on the scene and gallantly carried their enemies from this exposed, hopeless position, putting them ashore on the wild coast near Yarmouth. *Lively*'s captain was later relieved of his command for his humanitarian gesture.

The adventures of *Blonde*'s crew were not over, however. From Yarmouth they embarked in an open shallop for the dockyard at Halifax. En route they were picked up by the *Observer*, a coastal protection brig. As *Observer* entered the approaches to the capital on May 28 she was spotted by an American privateer, the cutter *Jack*, 15 guns, 58 men, under the command of the veteran seaman David Ropes. Ropes undoubtedly knew the *Observer*, but didn't reckon on her complement being augmented by *Blonde*'s rescued men. He attacked the brig, opening a fierce combat that lasted more than two hours. Both vessels fired broadsides, and each repeatedly tried to board the other.

Ropes did not live to see the battle's end. He was killed by *Observer*'s opening broadside. Their commander dead, *Jack*'s officers remained resolute, motivating their wavering crew

Halifax Harbour from King's Lime Yard. Early in the war, the naval dockyard itself was subject to suspicious arsons.

with accounts of the horrors awaiting them in prison ships if they were taken. Even this was insufficient against superior numbers, however. *Jack* finally struck her colours and, shattered, was taken into Halifax. The captured cutter was a welcome victory for British forces in Nova Scotia's privateering war.

By the spring of 1783 American privateering attacks on Nova Scotia at last ceased, but the American Revolutionary War's effect on the colony was far from over. The New England settlers of Liverpool, Cornwallis and Halifax were embittered and alienated by the wanton destruction perpetrated by their American cousins. Nova Scotia's economy was devastated by the war and would soon be further strained by the influx of thousands of desperate Loyalist refugees. In at least one way, however, the war had prepared the colony's people for the future. In response to relentless American attacks, some colonists — particularly those in Halifax and Liverpool — outfitted and manned privateers themselves. The skills learned during the Revolution would be put to good use when Nova Scotia again went to war, first with revolutionary France and then, once again, with the United States.

Chapter Nine

NOVA SCOTIANS ON THE SPANISH MAIN

On the fourth day of June, 1800, the loyal citizens of Liverpool, Nova Scotia celebrated the birthday of their king, George III, in style — by sending a fine new brig off to the Spanish Main on the first of what promised to be many profitable voyages. In the 17 years since the end of the American Revolutionary War, Liverpool had grown from a besieged village battered by repeated raids, to a prosperous and confident town whose fishers and merchants embarked on trading voyages of hundreds of miles, exchanging fish and timber for the products of the south — sugar, rum and salt. Loyalist refugees had swollen Liverpool's population, contributing skills and ingenuity to the development of the town's trade with the West Indies. Now, as France and Spain replaced American colonial rebels as enemies in the latest conflicts following the great upheaval of the French Revolution, Liverpool's merchants, shipbuilders and seamen energetically re-embraced another familiar trade: privateering.

The fine brig that crossed the harbour bar that day, sailing south and east for steady winds of the Gulf Stream, was called *Rover*. Mounting 14 cannon, her crew of 55 armed with muskets, cutlasses, pikes and pistols, she was provisioned for a months-long voyage to the Caribbean in search of rich enemy prizes, and their cargoes of sugar, cocoa, rum, wine, tobacco and indigo. In command was Alexander Godfrey, an experienced seaman whose history matched that of Liverpool in the years since the American war. Godfrey was a Loyalist who came to Nova Scotia in 1784, settling in Herring Cove within sight of the bare ledge where HMS *Blonde* had driven the sinister *Duc de Choiseul* and her incendiary cargo ashore years before. For years Godfrey worked in Liverpool vessels, fishing as far north as Labrador and trading as far south as the coast of Venezuela — the fabled Spanish Main. He continued to sail in them when Britain declared war on France, ablaze with the fires of revolution, in 1793. Godfrey left the sea and established himself as a merchant in Liverpool in 1796, the very year that the town's West Indian trade collapsed, battered by an onslaught of French and Spanish privateers in distant southern seas.

Renewed war raised old fears in the British North American colonies and in Nova Scotia particularly. The young United States' sympathies were decidedly with

Commissioners House, in the Naval Yard, Halifax.

Halifax dockyard and Commissioner's House. In the late eighteenth and early nineteenth century, the dockyard would repeatedly host privateering vessels taking on guns, powder and shot, and other warlike provisions.

revolutionary France. This, coupled with the questioned loyalty of the French-speaking population, revived the ancient spectre of a two-pronged attack against Canada — overland from the south and up the St. Lawrence River. This time, it was feared a French army would besiege Quebec and a French navy would sail up the river. Farther east it was clear that Americans were abetting French privateers in the Atlantic, causing anxiety in Halifax that Nova Scotia would once again suffer privateers' depredations, and perhaps even those of a powerful expedition of the French navy.

This time, however, the strategic situation was far different. The French navy had been shattered by the Revolution: its aristocratic

Privateering brig Rover, *scene of Alex Godfrey's unlikely, lopsided victory on the Spanish Main.*

officer corps had been purged by radicals, its administration was ruined and its dockyards were in chaos. The British Royal Navy, led by brilliant seamen and driven by an unparalleled discipline, continued to rule the waves. In August 1796 Halifax was briefly rocked by the news that a French squadron had run a Royal Navy blockade and was sailing westward. When word arrived that it had merely landed at the outport of Bay Bulls, Newfoundland, burning a few houses and stores before sailing off again, its weakness was

made clear. It was soon evident that Nova Scotia itself was relatively secure from enemy attack. The colony's interests were vulnerable, however, hundreds of miles away in the West Indies, where dozens of French and Spanish privateers, small enough to evade Royal Navy patrols, were attacking British trading vessels, including those of Liverpool.

Liverpool responded to attacks on its commerce by mounting a commercial war, outfitting privateers to prey on French and Spanish enemies that threatened the town's lucrative West Indies trade. In 1798 Liverpool merchants launched *Charles Mary Wentworth*, a full-rigged ship named after the son of Nova Scotia's governor, Sir John Wentworth. Unlike the town's fledgling privateers of the American Revolutionary war, *Wentworth* was a big, powerful vessel, built to make long cruises in distant waters with a large crew and heavy armament. Her owners — prominent townsmen like Simeon Perkins, Joseph Barss Sr. and Joseph Freeman — voyaged to Halifax to obtain a privateering commission, as well as 16 cannon from the naval dockyard to serve as teeth on her imminent cruise.

Charles Mary Wentworth embarked on her first cruise on August 15, 1798, soon taking a Spanish brigantine bound from Havana with a cargo of cotton, cocoa and sugar. She then recaptured an American brig from the French, before returning to Liverpool on December 16. At dockside men sifted the brigantine's bulk cocoa for gold coins stowed there, perhaps, by the vessel's Spanish crew. *Wentworth*'s prizes were the first of dozens of vessels taken by Nova Scotian privateers in the wars with revolutionary and Napoleonic France and its allies.

On her next cruise to the West Indies *Wentworth* was joined by the privateer schooner *Fly*, initiating squadron actions that would characterize Liverpool privateering for the next two years. On this cruise the consorts took four prizes laden with brandy, wines and dry goods, including the Spanish

Sailor mending a sail, scrimshaw image of the everyday routines of shipboard life.

letter-of-marque schooner *Causilidad*. She in turn was sold to Shelburne interests, who outfitted her as the privateer brigantine *Lord Nelson*. Nova Scotia's privateering successes grew exponentially, as captured vessels were in turn outfitted for privateering and took further prizes. On her third cruise *Wentworth* captured *Nuestra Señora del Carmen*. She was re-rigged and launched as the privateer *Duke of Kent*, named for Prince Edward, then military commander at Halifax. *Kent* had a long and successful career, and on her very first cruise took the schooner *Lady Hammond*, which was outfitted as the privateer *Lord Spencer*.

When *Rover* left Liverpool in the first week of June 1800, she at first cruised alone, following the Gulf Stream south to the Puerto Rican coast, hunting in the shipping lanes joining Europe and the Spanish Main. Alexander Godfrey kept a keen watch, for both enemy shipping and the Royal Navy: a visit from a navy press gang might seriously reduce the size of his crew, perhaps even force him to abandon his cruise. On June 14 he sighted a convoy of six vessels which he soon determined to be a French privateer schooner and five of her prizes. The enemy privateer mounted 16 cannon, and several of the prizes were likewise armed. Regardless, Godfrey prepared to engage them.

The convoy scattered, forcing Godfrey to pick his targets and chase them down one by one. He chose the biggest, most promising ship first, forcing her French prize crew to surrender. This was an American whaling ship, *Rebecca*, of New Bedford, Massachusetts, captured by the French while inbound with 1100

Colour engraving of northern whale fishery. Whaling ships' cargoes, such as that taken by Rover, *might prove especially valuable.*

casks of valuable whale oil aboard. *Rover* resumed the hunt, retaking the brig *Moses Myers*, captured by the French en route to Boston from Madeira with a cargo of wines. While returning home the Liverpool men took another vessel, the sloop *General Green* en route to Curaçao with a contraband cargo. On July 4, exactly one month after her departure, *Rover* returned to Liverpool with her three prizes. In his diary for the day, Simeon Perkins noted that the town was loud with the sound of privateersmen drinking and fighting, celebrating the opening success of this fateful little ship.

It was Godfrey's second cruise in *Rover*, however, that won both man and ship immediate and lasting fame. After a brief sojourn in port, during which the ship's battery was raised to 16 cannon and a larger crew of 60 men was shipped, *Rover* left port on July 17, within a week of her fellow-privateers *Charles Mary Wentworth* and *Duke of Kent*. Eager for prizes Godfrey shaped a southward course, cruising the waters where he had shattered the French privateer's convoy little more than a month earlier.

Finding no prizes this time Godfrey worked the ship deeper into the islands, provisioning at the Virgin Islands before cruising off Puerto Rico and through the Mona Passage, from the Atlantic to the Caribbean Sea. Still he found nothing. Increasingly, it threatened to be a disastrous season for all three privateers: *Charles Mary Wentworth* gave up the hunt, taking a humble salt cargo back to Nova Scotia; *Duke of Kent* returned home with less than nothing, after losing 20 of her men to Royal Navy press gangs; and by the end of August *Rover* was sailing off the Spanish Main between the ports of La Guaira and Puerto Cabello, contenting herself with the meagre cargoes of cocoa and salt she took from the small, open boats of the Spanish coastwise trade.

An enemy privateer working close inshore within sight of Spanish towns could not pass unobserved, however. Soon enemy authorities laid a trap for *Rover*, and on the morning of September 9, 1800 Godfrey sailed into it. Spotting a merchant schooner heading out from land he gave chase, following the smaller vessel as she altered course and headed back towards the safety of the coast. Prize crews and illness had reduced *Rover*'s strength to about 40 men, but surely this was enough to take a small, unarmed trader, Godfrey reasoned.

As *Rover* approached the calm, windless waters in the lee of the mainland's cliffs, however, the trap was sprung. A large schooner mounting 12 cannon — *Santa Rita* — drew steadily away from the land, towed by three fast galleys under oars, each with cannon mounted in the bow. Soon they would cut off *Rover*'s line of retreat. Becalmed, facing four ships and more than 200 men off a distant and hostile shore, *Rover* seemed doomed.

As the Spanish vessels drew ever closer under oars, *Rover*'s sails hung limp in the still air. If *Santa Rita* and the galleys approached near enough to board the privateer they would overwhelm her. The Nova Scotians would be slaughtered or captured and sent to rot in a pestilential Caribbean prison. Godfrey ordered his ship's long oars — her sweeps — broken out. Even so, there was no hope that the big privateer could out-row sleek galleys driven by slaves chained at their oars. *Rover*'s survival now depended on one of two possibilities, both remote: the wind might rise, allowing her to claw off the coast into open water; or, against great odds she might, with skilful ship-handling and sheer boldness, outfight her numerically superior foe.

The first scenario was more likely, and indeed a squall soon blew off the land, pushing *Rover* to seaward. But the wind dropped as quickly as it rose, leaving *Santa Rita* close off *Rover*'s stern, almost in firing range. As the Spanish schooner approached the privateer, firing at her rigging to cripple her, *Rover*'s crew readied for action under Godfrey's command. On one side of the vessel men tended the cannon, on the other they readied the sweeps to manoeuvre the ship. *Santa Rita* came ever closer, her bow crowded with eager men, armed

A twentieth-century photograph of Morro Castle, at the entrance of Havana harbour, Cuba. The fort was originally built in the late sixteenth century to protect the town from buccaneering attacks.

allowing *Rover*'s men to retrain their guns and fire on the open vessels at close range. The galleys' mangled crews rowed their damaged vessels out of range.

The wind rose again, now blowing off the sea and pushing the combatants ever closer to the high cliffs of the Spanish Main. *Santa Rita*'s foretopmast, damaged in the fight, came crashing down on the bloodstained deck below, rendering the ship briefly unmanageable. A rising swell made it ever more difficult to manoeuvre the damaged galleys. *Rover* now had a clear chance to escape offshore. Instead, Godfrey pressed home his assault, heedless of the odds against him.

and ready to leap aboard and avenge themselves on the men who dared prey on their trade.

As the Spaniards tensed for the assault, Godfrey gave his order. The sweeps bit into the calm water, spinning *Rover* around so her primed cannon faced the unsuspecting attackers. In an instant match met fuse and a fatal hail of jagged metal drove into *Santa Rita*'s boarders, shambling the deck with torn and screaming men and shattered gear. Godfrey shifted the sweeps to *Rover*'s opposite side and they bit again, bringing the ship's other broadside to bear, stunning the mauled Spanish ship and crew. Seeing the carnage on their sister, the galleys halted their advance,

Letting the wind carry his ship towards *Santa Rita*, Godrey ordered his crew to maintain a steady fire on the enemy's deck: grapeshot from the cannon and musketry from sharpshooters in *Rover*'s rigging. As the two ships closed, the galleys again rowed to *Santa Rita*'s aid. Before they arrived within range, Godfrey and two dozen of his men boarded the Spanish schooner, fighting their way through the bloody debris of the damaged ship's deck with pistols, pikes and cutlasses. The stunned Spanish sailors and marines succumbed to the privateersmen, hauling down their ensign in token of surrender. When the galleys saw the schooner lost they hauled off, unwilling to suffer further at the hands of an enemy now manning *Santa Rita's* 12 cannon in addition to *Rover's* 16. Through sheer boldness and tactical intelligence, Godfrey and his men had prevailed against an overwhelming force fighting in its home waters.

It was soon clear that *Rover's* opening broadsides had devastated the Spaniards, killing and maiming dozens in *Santa Rita* and breaking the will to fight. In all 54 of the enemy were dead, including all but one of the schooner's officers, and another 71 were taken prisoner. Amazingly, *Rover* did not suffer a single casualty, dead or injured. By mid-September damage to the privateer and her prize had been repaired, and putting most of his prisoners ashore, Godfrey sailed for home on September 14.

Making landfall on October 16, Godfrey and his crew caused a sensation in Liverpool. Word of their bold exploits soon passed from the South Shore town to Halifax, where the capital buzzed with accounts of their unlikely triumph. Within weeks news reached London where the story was broadcast in the definitive *Naval Chronicle*, the names of the humble Nova Scotian privateersmen appearing alongside those of Britain's greatest commanders in the interminable wars with France.

Alexander Godfrey, like John Rous before him, was offered a Royal Navy commission in recognition of his bravery and ability as captain of a private man-of-war. Unlike Rous he declined it, preferring a spell ashore after his two cruises. When *Rover* next sailed she was under a different master, the 24-year-old Joseph Barss Jr., later to gain fame in the brilliantly successful *Liverpool Packet*. His success in *Rover*, however, was decidedly modest. Departing Nova Scotia in January 1801, he took a small Spanish schooner in the Mona Passage and intercepted two American sloops carrying contraband cargoes off the coast of Puerto Rico. In June, Godfrey took the ship to the Caribbean once more, returning to Liverpool on September 5 without a single prize. French and Spanish prey had, for the time being, been hunted out.

In 1802 and 1803 a brief peace, the Peace of Amiens, gave the contesting forces an opportunity to regroup and rebuild in anticipation of the continuing warfare that lay before them. Liverpool's peacetime trade with the West Indies rebounded: even the fierce *Rover* carried humble cargoes of fish and timber southward along the Gulf Stream. When the fight resumed, Nova Scotians returned to privateering, with unspectacular results. Spain did not immediately rejoin the war, and French prizes remained scarce. Britain grew increasingly eager to retain the good will of the United States, and Vice Admiralty courts grew increasingly reluctant to condemn captured American vessels carrying cargoes that, according to the privateers that took them, belonged to the enemy.

Coupled with the actions of unwise captains, this new situation proved disastrous for the owners of some privateering vessels. In 1803 *Rover* undertook one last cruise to the south, this time under the less than scrupulous Benjamin Collins. Through the late summer and autumn he took Spanish and American ships, sending them northwards with prize crews, heedless of the protestations of innocence offered by their masters. The Spanish brig *Lanzarote*, carrying a cargo of sugar and molasses from Havana, proved an illegitimate capture at the Court of Vice Admiralty, exposing *Rover's* owners to charges of piracy and resulting in a large damage award against them. The two American captures were repatriated without ever reaching Nova Scotian waters.

The days of spectacular returns on privateering investment were, for a time, past. When *Duke of Kent* returned to Liverpool on August 18, 1805, it was the last time a Nova Scotian privateer cruised against an enemy for seven years. Privateering resumed in 1812 with renewed ferocity against a different but very familiar enemy. Alexander Godfrey would not be among the bold Nova Scotians who sailed out in this war, however. He died at sea of yellow fever at the end of 1804, and was buried ashore in the British colony of Jamaica.

Chapter Ten

NEW ENGLAND'S SCOURGE

On a raw November day in 1811, Enos Collins joined his fellow merchants in the warmth and bustle of a Halifax tavern, the Spread Eagle, for an auction of prize vessels condemned by the city's Court of Vice Admiralty. Halifax thrived during the seemingly interminable conflict between Britain and Napoleonic France, growing rich on huge profits from illicit trade with the New England states, and serving as a western Atlantic base for Royal Navy ships enforcing a blockade of the French enemy. Prize auctions were a common event in Halifax, but the vessel offered for sale this day was exotic even by the standards of a town sometimes glutted with captured brigs, schooners, snows, sloops and cutters — the many and varied rigs of all the Atlantic nations.

Black Joke was a fast, compact, sharp-bowed schooner of a type increasingly common on the United States' Chesapeake Bay, a type soon to win lasting fame as blockade-runners and

privateers. She was built for speed to serve in the most ignoble of ocean trades, as a tender to a ship carrying enslaved Africans to the Americas. *Black Joke* was captured by Royal Navy ships enforcing the blockade and the ban on slave trading, a practice outlawed by Britain in 1807. When she arrived in Halifax she still reeked of the horrors that had transpired in her below-decks. Before she was turned to legal trades her new owners had to fumigate her with vinegar, tar and brimstone.

Those new owners were Enos Collins and his Liverpool, Nova Scotia partners: Benjamin Knaut and John and James Barss. Collins had recently established himself as a merchant in Halifax, having gained broad experience in trading and privateering as a young man in

Enos Collins, privateering officer, shipowner, merchant and banker. Collins was one of the driving forces behind Nova Scotia's privateering enterprise in the early nineteenth century.

Left: Collins' Bank, Historic Properties, Halifax: one of the most concrete legacies of privateering in Nova Scotia.
Right: A modern weather vane testifies to Liverpool's privateering past.

Liverpool. A merchant and seaman of long experience, he had gone to sea as a boy in fishing and merchant vessels, rising to serve as First Lieutenant in the privateer *Charles Mary Wentworth*.

Speculation soon arose about the trade to which Collins' new purchase would be turned. She was small — barely more than 50 feet long, and narrow — with little room for Nova Scotia's standard bulk cargoes of codfish or timber. She was clearly ill suited to either the fisheries or to merchant trading. Nevertheless, Collins soon had her carrying passengers and cargo from Halifax to his old hometown, on a regularly scheduled service reflected in her new name: *Liverpool Packet*.

Her new trade did not end speculation, however. Collins

Portrait of Liverpool Packet. *The most famous and successful of Nova Scotia's many privateers, she terrorized the New England coast in the War of 1812.*

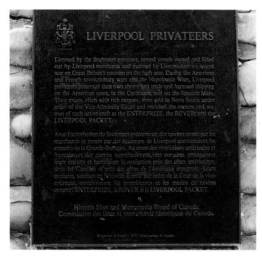

National Historic Sites and Monuments Board's monument to Liverpool's privateering heritage.

The US privateer brig Grand Turk, *1815. A dedicated, formidable small private ship-of-war.*

was known for his canniness and foresight, and many felt the sharp little schooner was ideally suited to chase and capture enemy shipping as a privateer. She was too small for the six-month Caribbean cruises against French and Spanish shipping Liverpool privateers had undertaken earlier, but she was well suited for action against a looming enemy nearer at hand: the United States. In 1811 Britain and the United States were still at peace, but tensions had been rising for years, inflaming passions cooled but not extinguished since the end of the American Revolutionary War, some 25 years earlier. They now threatened to break out in renewed conflict.

The Royal Navy's long, blockade of France was Britain's chief weapon in the fight against Napoleon's Grand Army, then marching triumphantly across Europe. Britain couldn't match Napoleon on land, but could starve his forces of the supplies he needed to sustain his imperial conquests. The United States, as the main neutral nation supplying France, suffered the routine brutality and inconvenience of the blockade. The Royal Navy boarded hundreds of American ships and hundreds of cargoes were seized. For Britain, sustaining the blockade was enormously difficult and costly: at the outset of the war in 1793 the Royal Navy could muster 135 ships and some 45,000 seamen; by 1812 the tally was 620 ships and 145,000 seamen.

The Royal Navy's insatiable need for crews to man its ships dramatically heightened tensions with the United

Reproduction of an early nineteenth-century privateer's costume and flintlock.

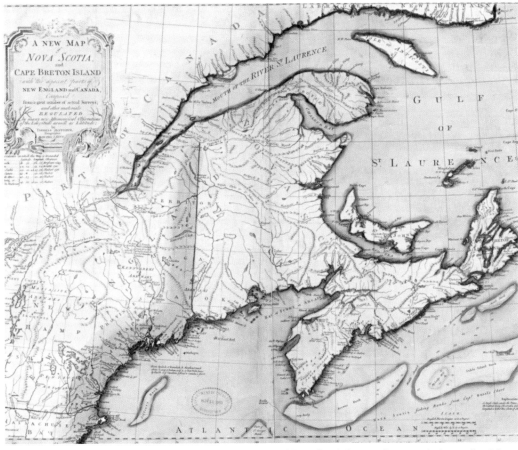

A contemporary map of the Atlantic Provinces showing Nova Scotia's tempting proximity to the rich ports of the United States' eastern seaboard.

States. British naval vessels stopped and boarded American merchant vessels in mid-ocean, pressing sailors into hard, dangerous service in the lower decks of His Majesty's ships. Protests that the pressed men were American citizens carried little weight against British assertions that once the king's subject, a man was always the king's subject. So soon after the Revolutionary War, this meant in practice that any United States citizen over the age of thirty was considered a Briton, subject to impressment.

Thousands of Americans found themselves unwilling servants of a foreign sovereign. On June 22, 1807, HMS *Leopard* out of Halifax encountered the United States frigate

HMS Atalante, *a British navy frigate, in the approaches to Halifax harbour.*

Britain, creating a tremendous growth of smuggling in the northern states that enriched Canada, New Brunswick and Nova Scotia. While not ceasing to impress American seamen, Britain tried to avoid open conflict. To no avail: on June 18, 1812 the United States declared war on Great Britain. Nine days later HMS *Belvidera* entered Halifax Harbour with three American prizes in tow after encountering USS *President* and *Constitution* in the Atlantic, announcing open warfare to the bustling naval town. Even then, Britain remained reluctant to engage its familiar enemy. But not so the privateering merchants and seamen of Nova Scotia.

Chesapeake at sea off the American coast. Certain that the frigate had Royal Navy deserters aboard, *Leopard*'s captain ordered *Chesapeake* to stand by and be searched. *Chesapeake*'s captain refused. *Leopard* opened fire, loosing three broadsides, killing three men and wounding 18 in *Chesapeake*, including the frigate's captain. *Leopard*'s men then boarded *Chesapeake* and took off four sailors, returning them to Halifax for courts martial.

The American public in New York, Philadelphia and Baltimore — less so in Boston — were outraged. A clamour for war arose, finally to be satisfied five years later. American presidents Jefferson and Madison embargoed trade with

By July, American privateers were seen lurking off the Atlantic coast and in the Bay of Fundy. Remembering the bitter experience of the American Revolutionary War, Nova Scotians were eager to put to sea against their old enemy. The first vessel to enter the fray was the ex-slaver *Liverpool Packet*. By August, Collins and his partners were in Halifax petitioning the governor for a letter-of-marque, receiving a cautious and rather disingenuous commission to take French, rather than American, prizes. The schooner received a small but powerful battery of five cannon at the naval dockyard, supplementing this with 25 muskets, 40 cutlasses and

Cannon pointing out over Liverpool harbour at Fort Point.

provisions for a two-month cruise. At the end of August, with Captain John Freeman and a crew of 45 men aboard, she departed Liverpool on her inaugural privateering cruise.

Liverpool Packet sailed southwards and cruised Georges Bank, off the Massachusetts coast, aiming to intercept American shipping inbound from Europe to Boston and other New England ports. These were familiar waters for Nova Scotian seamen, and their hopes were soon fulfilled: on September 7 they took the merchant vessel *Middlesex* with a cargo of coal, salt and earthenware, sending her into Halifax

Eighteenth-century bell from the naval dockyard in Halifax: the dockyard played an essential role in outfitting Nova Scotia's privateers.

to have her legitimacy as a prize judged at the Court of Vice Admiralty. Her next prize, *Factor*, had had her cargo of wine picked over by a British privateer, but sufficient remained in her hold to treat *Packet*'s crew.

Captures came thick through September and early November: *Polly*, bound from Charleston to Boston with a cargo of rice; *Union*, Philadelphia to Bath, Maine with flour and corn; *Four Brothers*, Thomaston, Maine to Boston; *Anson*, Boston to Baltimore; *Little Joe*, Boston to New York. *Liverpool Packet* returned to port on October 19, having cut a swath through the coastwise trade of the United States on her first cruise.

Portrait of Joseph Barss, Jr., master of Liverpool Packet, Nova Scotia's most famous and successful privateer.

On her next cruise *Liverpool Packet* sailed under the veteran command of Joseph Barss, Jr., brother of two of her owners. Barss first went to sea as a teenager, working on his father's vessels in Liverpool's Labrador fisheries. When his hometown made war on French and Spanish shipping in the Caribbean, Barss sailed as Second Lieutenant in *Charles Mary Wentworth* and then as captain of *Lord Spencer*. In 1801 he succeeded Alexander Godfrey as commander of the famed *Rover*. By 1812 Barss was already a proven privateering captain. His successes in *Liverpool Packet* would make him a legend.

Barss immediately returned the ship to New England waters, cruising first on Georges Bank and then moving closer inshore, hunting the waters adjacent to Cape Cod and Massachusetts Bay. Here American coastwise shipping routes

A company of soldiers musters at Liverpool's "Privateer Days" celebration.

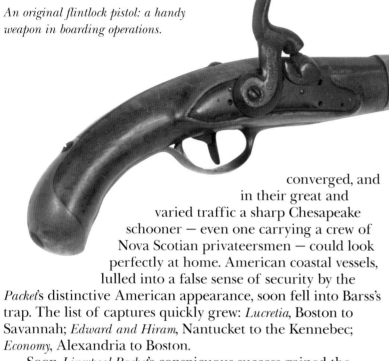

An original flintlock pistol: a handy weapon in boarding operations.

converged, and in their great and varied traffic a sharp Chesapeake schooner — even one carrying a crew of Nova Scotian privateersmen — could look perfectly at home. American coastal vessels, lulled into a false sense of security by the *Packet*'s distinctive American appearance, soon fell into Barss's trap. The list of captures quickly grew: *Lucretia*, Boston to Savannah; *Edward and Hiram*, Nantucket to the Kennebec; *Economy*, Alexandria to Boston.

Soon *Liverpool Packet*'s conspicuous success gained the attention of the New England press. Newspapers inflated the ship's captures, portraying Barss and his crew as a menace rivalling the legendary French corsair Morpain, scourge of the Massachusetts coast a hundred years earlier. Public anger grew, stoked by rumours that Barss was an American traitor whose depredations merited the severest punishment. Instruments of vengeance soon appeared, as the citizens of Boston and Salem outfitted vessels to hunt Barss and his ship. But they could not halt the litany of captures along the New England coast: *Chase*, Portland to Norfolk; *Dove*, Philadelphia to Gloucester; *Three Friends*, Baltimore to Boston. The toll on coastal shipping became so great that New Englanders talked of cutting a canal through the base of Cape Cod, saving

vessels the need to sail around its sandy point under the eyes of ravening privateers.

American shipping finally enjoyed a respite in the winter of 1812-13, in part because *Liverpool Packet* was laid up in Nova Scotia refitting after the hard cruising of the previous year. In early March she sailed south once again, in consort with fellow privateers *Retaliation* and *Sir John Sherbrooke*.

This time, her reputation preceded her: hearing rumours of *Liverpool Packet*'s presence, many vessels promptly returned to port. Others did not hear the warning, or did not heed it. Barss and his crew took more than a dozen American ships before returning to Nova Scotia, this time to Halifax, in late May. This cruise was Barss's most successful but also his riskiest. In mid-April *Liverpool Packet* narrowly escaped capture — twice — by American privateers, first by the *New Orleans* and then by the *Little Duck* out of Falmouth. In each case Barss had relied on *Packet*'s fast lines to outrun the Americans under sweeps, barely escaping after tremendous effort. It proved a grim foreshadowing for Barss and his crew.

Liverpool Packet next left Nova Scotia on June 8, 1813 on a cruise that ended almost as soon as it began. On the eleventh Barss spotted a vessel at anchor along the Maine coast. As he approached and prepared to engage, it became clear that his prey was an enemy, and armed. The vessel was the privateer *Thomas*, 10 carriage guns, 4 swivels, out of Portsmouth, New Hampshire. Barss tried to run, throwing most of his cannon overboard to lighten ship. *Thomas* chased and closed with the *Packet*, firing her big guns. Barss saw capture was now inevitable and struck his colours. Regardless, *Thomas*'s men boarded her with musket fire, initiating an exchange that killed men on both sides.

The Nova Scotian vessel was secured and carried back to Portsmouth, where its crew faced the noisy threats of a mob enraged at the blood spilled in the action. They were cast in jail and Captain Barss, whose reputation had dogged New England's fleets for months, was treated with especial harshness, kept alive on a meagre diet of water and hard bread.

Liverpool Packet did not remain idle for long. Her fine lines soon attracted New England buyers, who again outfitted her for privateering. One of these was Captain William Dobson who renamed her *Young Teazer's Ghost* in memory of his former ship, hunted down and spectacularly destroyed in Nova Scotia's Mahone Bay. She was then sold to Captain John Perkins, who tauntingly renamed her *Portsmouth Packet* and sent her cruising against British interests. In October 1813 she left her homeport and cruised northwards towards the Bay of Fundy. On the fifth she encountered the Royal Navy brig *Fantôme* off Maine's Mount Desert Island. She ran, but was taken after a 13-hour chase. Brought before the Halifax Court of Vice Admiralty she was again condemned and sold at auction. Again she was purchased by Enos Collins.

By the end of November *Liverpool Packet* had her old name restored, a new letter of marque and a new commander. Caleb Seely was an experienced officer, master of the privateer schooner *Star* out of Saint John. He soon demonstrated his worth. After a month-long cruise he returned to Nova Scotia with a number of American coasting vessels taken in familiar waters off Block Island. In January 1814 he sailed again in company with *Retaliation*, ranging southward to the shores of Connecticut and Long Island Sound. In the course of his two cruises in the *Packet* Seely took at least 14 prizes. The New England press again decried depredations wrought by the

Re-enactors representing American rebel forces get a warmer welcome than their attacking ancestors did at Liverpool's "Privateer Days."

little Nova Scotian ship, but apparently found Seely's character more to their liking than Barss's. His gallant conduct was roundly praised.

Liverpool Packet undertook one last cruise in the autumn of 1814 under the commander of Seely's former prize master, Lewis Knaut, who managed to send in at least another four prizes before the ship closed its privateering career at year's end. In two years of war 44 vessels taken by *Liverpool Packet* had been successfully condemned at the Court of Vice

Admiralty. She had captured at least 60 and perhaps as many as 100 in total. The foul-smelling vessel with the ignominious past proved herself as Nova Scotia's most brilliantly successful privateer of the War of 1812.

Her most successful master, however, Joseph Barss Jr., remained imprisoned in Portsmouth for months despite the efforts of influential friends like Enos Collins, who petitioned John Coape Sherbrooke, lieutenant-governor of Nova Scotia, to intercede on the privateer's behalf. When he was finally released on parole Barss returned to the sea, making a voyage to the West Indies in an armed trader named *Wolverine*. Amazingly this was the former Portsmouth privateer *Thomas*, which had captured him in 1813. She in turn was captured and renamed in late 1813. Soon after this trip Barss retired from the sea for good, buying a farm in the Annapolis Valley near Kentville in 1817. There he died in 1824, attended by his wife and many children, far from the tumult of Nova Scotia's privateering wars.

A reproduction of an eighteenth-century general-use sundial compass.

Chapter Eleven

NOVA SCOTIA'S MAN O' WAR

On May 27, 1813 the brig *Sir John Sherbrooke*, Nova Scotia's largest and most powerful private armed vessel, was cruising off the New England coast when she closed with the *General Plumer*, an American privateer. As a rule privateers from warring nations avoided one another at sea, preferring instead to prey on fat, unarmed merchantmen. This day, however, *Sherbrooke's* crew felt confident of the outcome. Their ship carried 18 cannon and a crew of 150, including 50 marines armed with 50 muskets and 80 cutlasses. The *General Plumer* carried only six cannon, many of her crew were away on prizes taken during a three months' cruise and the ship was crammed with English and Irish prisoners captured from the brig *Duck* the day before. *Sherbrooke* captured the American privateer after a quick fight.

Two days later *Sherbrooke* met the trim, powerful Royal Navy frigate HMS *Shannon* near Cape Anne off the New England coast.

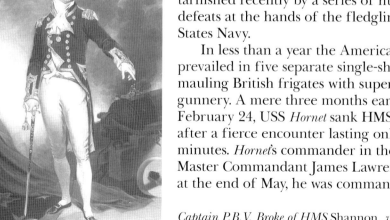

Shannon's men boarded *Sherbrooke* and pressed 20 or so of *Duck's* Irishmen, drilling them for imminent action. *Shannon's* Captain, P.B.V. Broke, was embarked on a cruise with a two-fold mission: to enforce the blockade of United States' ports and to brighten the honour of the Royal Navy, tarnished recently by a series of humiliating defeats at the hands of the fledgling United States Navy.

In less than a year the Americans had prevailed in five separate single-ship duels, mauling British frigates with superior gunnery. A mere three months earlier, on February 24, USS *Hornet* sank HMS *Peacock* after a fierce encounter lasting only 14 minutes. *Hornet's* commander in the fight was Master Commandant James Lawrence. Now, at the end of May, he was commander of USS

Captain P.B.V. Broke of HMS Shannon, *victor of one of the most famous frigate duels of all time.*

Shannon *and* Chesapeake *engaged in battle: Nova Scotian privateers played an unexpected role in* Shannon*'s victory.*

Shannon leading her prize, Chesapeake triumphantly into Halifax Harbour.

flags." Shortly after noon, as a boat crew still rowed towards the harbour with his challenge, Broke saw *Chesapeake* loosing sail and getting under way. Boston's rooftops and waterfront were packed with spectators, the harbour swarmed with yachts and small craft carrying townspeople eager to witness another glorious victory for American arms. As the ship passed Boston Lighthouse and set a course for the waiting *Shannon*, her long white pennant trailed the motto "Free Trade and Sailors' Rights" in the warm breeze.

All through the afternoon the two warships engaged in a slow stately dance, as they manoeuvred into position to engage one another. By 5:50 p.m. they had closed to within 50 yards. *Shannon* opened fire, loosing a devastating broadside that killed *Chesapeake*'s helmsmen. The American ship continued to drift forward, exposing her vulnerable stern to the Royal

Chesapeake at Boston, preparing for a Mediterranean cruise. As the ship's crew worked to ready her for sea they could see Broke's *Shannon* cruising off the harbour mouth, daring them to come out and fight.

On the first of June — a fine, clear morning with a breeze off the land — Broke penned a gallant challenge to Lawrence, inviting *Chesapeake* to come out and face *Shannon* in single combat, "ship to ship, to try the fortunes of our respective

A naval cutlass of the early nineteenth century: a weapon used in hand-to-hand combat.

Navy gunners' raking fire. A storm of flying iron and jagged wood splinters mangled the American gun crews below decks. The ships drifted together and struck. Broke ordered them lashed together. The commander himself then took a party of boarders against the shocked, desperate men on *Chesapeake*'s shambled decks, receiving several wounds before the Americans finally surrendered. Fifteen chaotic minutes after the battle began, British sailors hauled down *Chesapeake*'s flag and replaced it with a British ensign. Days later *Shannon* led the battered *Chesapeake* into Halifax before the delighted eyes of the thronging townspeople. The Royal Navy's honour, once challenged, was restored.

It was only fitting that *Sir John Sherbrooke* stood by to assist *Shannon* on the eve of her epic battle with *Chesapeake*. Originally built as the Marblehead, Massachusetts privateer *Thorn*, she was captured by the frigate HMS *Tenedos* in 1812, condemned, and sold to Liverpool owners including Enos Collins, Benjamin

Halifax-born Provo Wallis served as a lieutenant on Shannon *during her fight with* Chesapeake; *he later rose to the rank of Admiral of the Fleet in the Royal Navy.*

Knaut, John and Joseph Barss. She was much larger than other vessels owned by these experienced privateersmen, and was more heavily armed and crewed. Her captain, Joseph Freeman, was a colonel in the Queens County militia who had commanded the Liverpool privateers *Charles Mary Wentworth, Nymph* and *Duke of Kent* a decade earlier in the long wars with France and Spain, maintaining a high standard of discipline among his crews. Of all the Nova Scotian privateers in the War of 1812, *Sherbrooke* was perhaps the most martial, the best suited to serve alongside the disciplined crews of the Royal Navy.

Thorn was renamed in honour of Nova Scotia's governor, Sir John Sherbrooke, receiving her letter of marque on February 11, 1813. She departed on her first cruise in mid-March, joining her sisters *Retaliation* and *Liverpool Packet* in their ongoing campaign against the vulnerable American coastwise trade in the waters off Block Island, Massachusetts. *Sherbrooke* is said to have taken 14 vessels on this cruise: they included the *Frederick Augustus*, inbound from Cadiz with salt; the *Betsey* en route from Massachusetts to Havana carrying beef, pork, gin, tobacco and leather; and the *Fame* out of Newport, Rhode Island, carrying rum, brandy and mail to Manhattan.

In April *Sherbrooke* cruised in company with the Royal Navy sloop *Rattler* and the schooner *Bream*. The naval ships took eleven prizes during this cruise. None were attributed to *Sherbrooke* and none aboard received prize money from them. She next sailed with *Liverpool Packet*, in pursuit of the American privateer *Fox*, then known to be lurking off Nova Scotia's Atlantic Coast and Bay of Fundy. In the War of 1812 the colony was spared the privateering depredations that had characterized the American Revolutionary War. Nevertheless, American privateers did occasionally cruise the colony's familiar waters, sometimes to their peril. *Fox* managed to elude the Liverpool vessels, escaping across the Atlantic. Others were not so lucky.

Late in April *Sherbrooke* recaptured the schooner *Paulina* from a prize crew off the *General Plumer*, foreshadowing the capture of *Plumer* herself and the fierce battle of HMS *Shannon* and USS *Chesapeake*. *Sherbrooke* returned to home waters with her prizes and in June cruised the Nova Scotia coast, pursuing enemy privateers in the approaches to Halifax harbour. Late in the month she fell in with the New York privateer *Young Teazer*, commanded by Captain William Dobson, apparently chasing her right into the harbour itself, before leaving her to the care of the town's guns and those of the ships in the dockyard.

This wasn't *Young Teazer*'s the first close call in Nova Scotian waters, nor was it her last. A big, fast schooner distinguished by a fearsome alligator-shaped figurehead, she prowled the coast under the very eyes of colonial patrol brigs and Royal Navy ships. Rumours and legends swirled about this ship: that a huge reward was offered for her capture; and that she had Royal Navy deserters aboard; that her lieutenant,

Chest salvaged from the defeated Chesapeake *and maintained in the Maritime Museum of the Atlantic in Halifax.*

Melville Island, site of a notorious and pestilential military prison, as seen from the Halifax shore.

Halifax harbour and approaches were closely watched during the War of 1812, and Young Teazer *'s escape from* Sherbrooke *here is remarkable. It would prove, however, to be a temporary respite.*

Frederick Johnson, went into action with a noose around his neck, terrorizing both the enemy and his own crew; and that Johnson himself was a deserter, who would rather die than be captured and subjected to British naval law and punishment. Deserters or not, all aboard the *Teazer* had reason to fear imprisonment in the fetid, disease-ridden prisons at Halifax's Melville Island and England's Dartmoor.

On June 27 the *Sherbrooke* was cruising off the town of Lunenburg when she again picked up *Young Teazer*'s track. Giving chase, she pursued the enemy privateer towards nearby Mahone Bay before losing her in the thick fog that regularly shrouds this coast in early summer. *Teazer* ran blindly towards another British vessel, the *Orpheus* and soon the frigate HMS *La Hogue* joined the chase. The American privateer ran in towards the coast, trying to evade capture among Mahone Bay's dozens of small islands. *La Hogue*

anchored at the mouth of the bay, cutting off escape to seaward. Shore militias, alerted to the privateer's presence, stood by to intercept attempts to escape overland. *Young Teazer*, it seemed, was trapped.

La Hogue launched her boats, carrying parties of armed men towards the cornered privateer. *Teazer*'s men had three reasonable courses of action open to them: they could engage the boat parties and fight to regain open water; they could run aground and hide in the thick bush of the adjacent countryside; or they could surrender. Their deliberations were cut short, however, by the rash action of Frederick Johnson. Motivated by fear, madness or plain malevolence, Johnson ran below decks to *Teazer*'s powder magazine. Touching an open flame to this explosive cargo, Johnson, the handsome schooner and her crew were blown to pieces in an instant.

Naval traffic under the bluffs of the southern approaches to Halifax harbour. Vessels like these penned Young Teazer *in the confines of Mahone Bay before her catastrophic destruction.*

A moment later the sea around the smoking hulk of the wrecked vessel was a stew of torn bodies and charred flesh. Of the 36 men on board *Young Teazer* that day, 28 were killed outright. The few survivors, among them Captain Dobson himself, struggled ashore on nearby Anshutz Island and were captured by farmer Martin Rafuse. When they had recovered, they were taken before magistrates at Lunenburg. Dobson was soon at sea again, this time in command of *Young Teazer's Ghost*, the Nova Scotian privateer *Liverpool Packet*, renamed after her capture off the New England coast. *Teazer's* remains were salvaged from the bottom of Mahone Bay, but the legend of the ill-fated American privateer endures: to this day *Teazer's* ghost is said to silently cruise the waters of Nova Scotia's South Shore, perpetually re-enacting her fiery destruction.

Even as she assisted at *Teazer's* end, the *Sherbrooke's* days as a privateer were also numbered. As the war continued it became increasingly difficult to sustain such a big ship and her big, hungry crew with the proceeds of small prizes gleaned from the American coastwise trade. In August 1813, after a spring's cruising season in which she took a total of 18 prizes, the privateer was offered for sale at Liverpool. Her new owners converted her into an armed merchant vessel, trading to the West Indies and Europe. On one such voyage, the American privateer *Syren* captured *Sherbrooke*, bound for Spain with a cargo of fish. Failing to get their prize home through the ever-tightening Royal Navy blockade, her captors set her ablaze — an undignified end for a warlike consort of naval brigs and frigates. Her captain, Joseph Freeman, had a rather more successful career after his cruising days, ultimately rising to become a member of the Nova Scotia legislature.

As the War of 1812 approached its end, so did the exciting, risky, and occasionally lucrative profession of privateering. A century later, when the nations of Europe and America again met in the Great War, privateering had long been outlawed by the 1856 Declaration of Paris. Soon, however, a new invention — the attack submarine — and a new naval power — Germany — resurrected the war on trade in a form more terrible than previously imagined. In the wars of the twentieth century Halifax harbour would again be crammed with ships, seeking Royal Navy protection as they crossed the North Atlantic with cargoes to feed the wars in Europe. Many would never arrive, their hulls torn open by explosive torpedoes on the high seas. The new century would have no time for the civilities of a Court of Vice Admiralty.

Today, only faint traces remain of the Maritimes' bold privateering past: rusting cannons planted muzzle down at small-town street corners, old wharf pilings slowly rotting into cold harbours and a few waterfront buildings that have survived two centuries of urban development. It is possible, however, that this vital period has left a more lasting legacy, a legacy exemplified by the careers of Enos Collins or Samuel Cunard — men who transformed privateering profits into immense fortunes and world-girdling businesses.

BIBLIOGRAPHY

The literature on privateering in Canada's Atlantic Provinces is a growing one, with new and innovative academic studies complementing older, swashbuckling romantic chronicles. I have relied on works of both sorts while researching and writing this book. The following is a list of some of the sources I've found most useful and interesting; readers wishing to learn more about the many facets of Canadian privateering may likewise find them helpful.

Bromley, John S. *Corsairs and Navies, 1660-1760.* London: Hambleton Press, 1987.

Chapin, Howard M. *Privateering in King George's War 1739-1748.* Providence, 1928.

Chard, Don. "The Impact of French Privateering on New England, 1689-1713." *American Neptune.* Vol. 35 (July 1975), pp.153-165.

Clarke, Ernest. *The Siege of Fort Cumberland, 1776: An Episode of the American Revolution.* Montreal: McGill-Queen's University Press, 1995

Conlin, Daniel. "A Private War in the Caribbean: Nova Scotia Privateering, 1793-1805." *The Northern Mariner,* Vol. VI, No. 4 (October 1996), pp. 29-46.

Crouse, Nellis M. *Lemoyne d'Iberville: Soldier of New France.* Toronto: Ryerson Press, 1954.

Douglas, W.A.B. "The Sea Militia of Nova Scotia, 1749-1766." *Canadian Historical Review,* Vol. XLVII (1966), pp. 22-37.

Johnston, A.J.B. *The Summer of 1744. A Portrait of Life in 18th Century Louisbourg.* Ottawa: Parks Canada, 1983.

Kert, Faye. *Prize and Prejudice: Privateering and Naval Prize in Atlantic Canada in the War of 1812.* St. John's, Nfld.: International Maritime Economic History Association, 1997.

Leefe, John. *The Atlantic Privateers: Their Story 1749-1815.* Halifax: Petheric Press, 1978.

Mullane, George. "The Privateers of Nova Scotia, 1756-1783." *Collections of the Nova Scotia Historical Society.* Vol. XX (1921), pp. 17-42.

Murdoch, Beamish. *A History of Nova Scotia, or Acadie.* Halifax, NS: J. Barnes, 1865-1867.

Nichols, George E.E. "Notes on Nova Scotian Privateers." *Collections of the Nova Scotia Historical Society.* Vol. XIII (1908), pp. 111-152.

Proulx, Jean Pierre. *The Military History of Placentia: A Study of the French Fortifications/Placentia, 1713-1811.* Ottawa: Parks Canada, 1979.

Pullen, H.J. *The Shannon and the Chesapeake.* Toronto: McClelland and Stewart, 1970.

Rawlyk, George A. *Yankees at Louisbourg.* Orono, ME: University of Maine Press, 1967.

Snider, C.H.J. *Under the Red Jack: Privateers of the Maritime Provinces in the War of 1812.* London: Martin Hopkinson & Co, 1928.

Swanson, Carl E. *Predators and Prizes: American Privateering and Imperial Warfare, 1739-1748.* Columbia, SC: University of South Carolina Press, 1991.

Webster, John Clarence. *Acadia at the End of the Seventeenth Century: Letters, Journals and Memoirs of Joseph Robineau de Villebon, Commandant of Acadia, 1690-1700, and Other Contemporary Documents.* Sackville, NB: Tribune Press, 1933.

INDEX

Abenaki, 33, 34, 37, 38, 40, 42
Acadians
  campaign against, 82-84
  expulsion of, 74, 80-82
Albany, 69, 70
Albany Fort, 15
Alexander, 66
Alfred, 91, 92
Alline, Henry, 94
American Revolutionary War
  British privateers, 90 92-93
  France and, 86-87
  Penobscot River battle, 93-94
  rebel privateering, 88-89, 91-92, 94-96
  rebel sympathy in Nova Scotia, 85-91
  sacking of Lunenburg, 95-96
Amherst, Jeffrey, 61-62
Amsterdam Post, 65
Andros, Edmund, 38
Annapolis Royal, 45, 76, 94
Anson, 112
Armateurs, 11-12
  See also Sea militias

Baptiste. *See* Maisonnat, Pierre
Barss, James, 105
Barss, John, 105
Barss, Joseph, Jr., 104, 112-115, 116
Barss, Joseph, Sr., 100, 120
Bart, Jean, 43
Beaubassin, 36, 39, 45, 70, 72
Beauchêne. *See* Chevalier, Robert
Beaumarchais, Pierre Augustin Caron de, 87
Belvidera, 110
Bergerac, 25
Betsey, 121
Betsy, 90
Black Joke, 105
Blockades, 74, 77, 108, 117, 125
Blonde, 85-86, 87, 93, 96
Boishébert, 70
Bonaventure, Simon-Pierre Denys de, 33
Boneto, 66
Bonhomme Richard, 92
Bonne, 31, 32
Boscawen, Admiral, 74, 82
Boston, 57
Boularderie, Antoine Le Poupet de la, 51-52
Bream, 121
Bridgar, John, 15
Broke, P.B.V., 117
Bromley, J.S., 47

Brouillan, Jacques-François de Mombeton de, 21
Brouillan, Joseph Mombeton de, 38

Callaghan, William, 93
Callbeck, Phillips, 89
Canadiens, 13-14
Canso, 53-55
Cantabre, 55-56
Caribou, 50
Causilidad, 100
César, 55-56
Chameau, 50
Charles Fort, 15
Charles Mary Wentworth, 100, 102, 112, 120
Charlottetown harbour, 89
Charmante, 32
Chase, 114
Chauffours, Marie-Charlotte d'Amours de, 41
Chauffours, Marie-Josèphe d'Amours de, 48
Chebeque, 60, 61
Chesapeake, 110
Chevalier, Robert, 46-47
Chignecto, 68-70, 72-73, 89
Chubb, Pascho, 33
Church, Benjamin, 39
Cobb, Sylvanus, 11, 76-77, 79, 81, 82-84
Collier, Sir George, 93
Collins, Benjamin, 104
Collins, Enos, 105-6, 115, 120, 125
Collin's Bank, 106
Compagnie du Nord, 11, 13, 15, 19
Corlaer raid, 18
Cornwallis, Edward, 75, 76
Corsairs, 9, 12
  See also Privateers
Coureurs de bois, 13
Craven, 15
Crowley, John, 6
Cunard, Samuel, 125

Dampier, William, 9, 47
D'Anville, Jean Baptiste Louis Frédéric de la Rochefoucauld de Roye, Duc, 58, 59-60, 68, 69
Dartmoor, 123
Davies, Thomas, 83
Davis, 93
Dawson, James, 90
Declaration of Paris, 125
De La Clara, 66
Dering, 22, 24

D'Iberville, Pierre Le Moyne, 10, 14-16, 18-24, 33, 34
Dobson, William, 115, 121, 125
D'Olabaratz, Joannis-Galand, 54-62
Dolphin, 95
Dove, 114
Dreadnought, 92
Duc de Choiseul, 86-87
Duck, 117
Duke of Kent, 100, 102, 104, 120
Dumaresq, Philip, 65
Du Vivier, Joseph Dupont, 54, 76

Economy, 114
Eddy, Jonathan, 90, 91
Edward and Hiram, 114
Eltham, 64
Enterprise, 92
Envieux, 31, 32, 33
Expulsion, of Acadians, 74, 80-81

Factor, 112
Fame, 121
Fantôme, 115
Fawson, Jones, 93
Flibustiers, 9, 11, 47
  See also Privateers
Fly, 100
Fort Beauséjour, 72, 75, 77-80, 90
Fort Cumberland, 90, 91
Fort Edward, 72
Fort Frederick, 88
Fort Laurence, 72, 75, 77
Fort Saint-Joseph, 34
Four Brothers, 112
Franklin, 89
Franklin, Benjamin, 67, 86
Frederick Augustus, 121
Freeman, John, 111
Freeman, Joseph, 100, 120, 125
French-English rivalry
  frontier warfare, 17-19
  in fur trade, 14-17
  King William's War, 17-24
  religious intolerance, 25-26
Frontenac, Louis Buade de, 16, 17
Fur trade, French-English rivalry in, 14-17

Gage, 93
General Green, 102
General Plumer, 117
Godfrey, Alexander, 97, 100, 102-4
Grand Banks fisheries, 20-21
Grymross, 83

Halifax, 71, 72, 98
  dockyards, 112
  founding of, 69
  harbour, 123, 124
  pro-American sympathies, 88
  threat of Rebel privateers, 91
Halifax Bob, 92
Hampshire, 22, 23-24
Hancock, 89
Havana, 83, 84
Hawk, 51
Hero, 95
Hope, 90
Hornet, 93
Hound, 77
How, Edward, 75
Howe, 93
Howe, William, 90, 91
Hudson's Bay, 22, 24
Hudson's Bay Company, 14-16

Île Royale, 49, 53-54
Impressment, 100, 102, 109-10, 117
Intrépide, 46
Iroquois, 15, 17

Jack, 96
James II, 16
Jefferson, Thomas, 110
Johnson, Frederick, 123
Jones, John Paul, 9192

King George's War, 50-52, 54-60
King William's War, 17-24
Kinsale, 53
Knaut, Benjamin, 105, 120
Knaut, Lewis, 116

La Corne, Chevalier, 70
La Hogue, 123
Lady Hammond, 100
Lanzarote, 104
La Rochelle, 59
La Salle, Robert Cavelier de, 23
Lawrence, Charles, 70
Lawrence, James, 117
LeDuff, Michel-Ange, 49
Le Loutre, Jean-Louis, 75-76
Leopard, 109-10
Little Duck, 114
Little Joe, 112
Lively, 93, 96
Liverpool, 86-88, 94, 97, 99-100
Liverpool Packet, 12, 104, 110-16, 120

Lizard, 87
Lord Nelson, 100
Lord Spencer, 100, 112
Louis XIV, 16, 25
Louisbourg, 36, 49-52, 54-58, 63-64, 68, 74, 76, 82-83
Louisiana, 23, 52
Loyal Briton, 88
Lucretia, 114
Lunenburg, 72, 77, 95-96
Lyon, James, 88

Machias, 88-89, 90, 91
Madison, James, 110
Madockawando, 38
Maisonnat, Pierre, 25-36, 42
    charged with piracy, 35-36
    commissioned, 30
    Pemaquid raid, 33-34
    prisoner in Boston, 29
    privateering activities, 29-36
    Protestant faith, 25
Malecite, 37
Manthet, Nicolas d'Ailleboust de, 18
Marguerite, 77
Maricourt, Paul Le Moyne de, 14
Marquis de Choiseul-Beaupré, 48
Mary, 66
Massachusetts, 64, 67, 68
Mather, Cotton, 26
Maugerville, 88, 90
Maurepas, Jean Frédéric Phélypeaux de, 54
Mediterranean galleys, 25, 26
Mellish, 91
Melville Island, 122, 123
Mermaid, 63-64
Middlesex, 111
Mi'kmaq, 33, 34, 37, 42, 48
Minas, 39, 74
Monckton, Robert, 77, 78-79, 82-84
Montcalm, Louis Joseph, Marquis de, 61, 74
Montreal, 15-17, 18
Moose Fort raid, 14-15, 15
Morpain, Pierre, 9, 42, 43, 46-52
Morro Castle, 103
Moses Myers, 102
Musketo, 5-6, 9
Musquodoboit, 70

Nancy, 50
Native peoples
    British allies, 15, 17
    French allies, 21, 33, 37, 40, 48
Naval Chronicle, 104

Nevis, 24
Newfoundland, French-English rivalry in, 20-22
New Orleans, 114
New York, 57
Nova Scotia
    American ties in, 85-86
    defence of, 92-93
    proximity to New England ports, 109
    rebel raids, 88-92, 94-96
    rebel sympathies in, 85-91
Nuestra Señora del Carmen, 100
Nymph, 120

Observer, 96
Orpheus, 123

Palmier, 22
Passamaquoddy, 88
Patience, 5-6
Paulina, 121
Peace of Amiens, 104
Peacock, 117
Pélican, 22-23
Pennell, Matthew, 6
Pentagouet, 38
Pepperell, William, 67
Perkins, John, 115
Perkins, Simeon, 87, 100, 102
Philadelphia, 57
Phips, Sir William, 28, 33, 76
Pidianske, 38
Plaisance, 20, 36, 42
Plymouth, 74
Polly, 88, 90, 112
Pontchartrain, Louis Phélypeaux de, 31, 32-33
Port Royal, 26, 29-39, 39-42, 45-46, 48
Portsmouth, England, 74
Portsmouth Packet, 115
Pemaquid raid, 20, 33-34
Prince of Orange, 56, 64
Privateers
    American rebel, 87-88, 91-96
    duties of, 11
    French Revolution, 97, 99
    King George's War, 55-57, 64-65, 67-68
    Queen Anne's War, 38-39, 41-44
    regulation of, 6
    relationship with regular naval service, 11
    on Spanish Main, 97-104
    spectrum of, 9-10
    state sponsorship of, 6, 8, 9
    War of 1812, 110-25

West Indian, 47
Profond, 33
Profond, 22
Providence, 91

Quebec, fall of, 60-62, 73
Queen Anne's War, 37-44
Queensbury, 50
Quesnel, Jean Baptiste Louis le Prévost du, 54

Rafuse, Martin, 125
Ranger, 51
Rangers, 83-84
Rattler, 121
Rebecca, 100
Renommée, 68
Retaliation, 114, 115, 120
Revenge, 92, 93
Revere, Paul, 93
Rhode Island, 57
Richardson, Captain, 51
Ronde, Louis Denys de la, 42
Ropes, David, 93, 96
Rous, John, 12, 64-74, 77, 80
Rover, 12, 97, 100-4
Royal Navy, 43, 93-94, 99, 100, 108-9, 117-20

Saint-Castin, Bernard-Anselme d'Abbadie de, 39-44
Saint-Castin, Jean-Vincent d'Abbadie de, 33, 37-38
Saint Christopher, 24
Saint-Domingue, 46, 47
Sainte-Hélène, Jacques Le Moyne de, 14, 18
St. Francis, 72
St. Jean Baptiste, 65
St. John's raid, 21-22
Salem, 56
Santa Rita, 102-4
Scammell, 95, 96
Schwartz, Magdalena, 95
Sea militias, 11-12
Seely, Caleb, 115, 116
Shannon, 117-20
Shirley, 64, 68, 69, 74
Shirley, Governor, 73
Sir George Collier, 92
Sir John Sherbrooke, 12, 114, 117, 120-21, 123-25
Smith, Stephen, 88
Soleil d'Afrique, 19
Soleil Royale, 33
Sorlings, 32
South Kingstown, 66

Squirrel, 83
Star, 115
Subercase, Daniel d'Auger de, 39, 41, 42, 46, 48
Succès, 50
Success, 92
Sulpicians, 16
Superbe, 64
Sutherland, 74
Swallow, 95
Syren, 125

Tenedos, 120
Thomas, 114
Thorn, 120
Three Brothers, 66
Three Friends, 114
Toulon, 57
Treaty of Aix-la-Chapelle, 62
Treaty of Ryswick, 24, 35
Tyng, Edward, 56-57, 64, 68

Ulysses, 83
Union, 112
Unity, 88
USS *Chesapeake*, 117-19, 121
USS *Constitution*, 110
USS *Hornet*, 117
USS *President*, 110

Vigilant, 63
Villebon, Joseph Robinau, 30, 32, 34, 35

Wallis, Provo, 120
War of Jenkin's Ear, 65
Warren, 81
Warren, Sir Peter, 10, 64, 68
Washington, 87
Washington, George, 88, 89, 91
Waterhouse, Samuel, 50-51
Wentworth, Sir John, 100
William of Orange, 17
Williams, John, 36
Winslow, John, 73-74, 77, 78, 80-82
Wolfe, James, 61, 74, 82

York, 76, 77, 81, 83
York Fort, 20, 22-23, 24
Young Eagle, 64-66
Young Teazer, 123-25
Young Teazer's Ghost, 115